For the legacy of

Vernon Grounds,

Eugene Peterson,

and Gaylord Kindschy.

My three pastors, mentors, and heroes

Ordinary Church

CONTENTS

Foreword

BY BRIAN ZAHND

Sometime in late modernity, Christians who had deeply, though mostly unwittingly, imbibed the heady cocktails served by the high priests of the Enlightenment (Voltaire, Hume, Nietzsche, et al.) conjured the drunken idea that Jesus had given a writ of divorce to the church. In an age of suspicion committed to the critique of tradition, how could it be otherwise? Surely the compelling figure of Jesus of Nazareth could have nothing to do with the tired institution that is dismissively referred to as "organized religion?" This secular assault upon the church found a surprising resonance among many Christians—especially pietists, revivalists, and rugged American individualists. Thus was born the modern idea of Jesus as personal savior (which really means private savior), leaving the church as little more than an optional common interest club for the more socially inclined. Jesus was essential, but the church was optional, or perhaps irrelevant, or even a hindrance to Christian faith.

Today this kind of thinking is in full bloom. But what should we make of it? Or perhaps a better question is, what would the first followers of Jesus make of this development? I have no doubt at all that they would scratch their heads at this strange new private religion with its stunning capacity to misunderstand Jesus and his message.

What was Jesus' message? What was his mission? Quite simply it was to inaugurate and establish the kingdom of God. Everything Jesus ever did—his preaching, his parables, his miracles, his table practice of radical hospitality—was an announcement and enactment of the kingdom of God. Jesus called upon those who heard his gospel announcement of the arrival of the kingdom of God to believe the message, rethink their lives, and to be baptized as a public testimony that they now belonged to this new way of being the people of God. Jesus was not offering private or postmortem salvation—Jesus was offering salvation as being personally gathered into the kingdom of God.

A close reading of the Gospels reveals that Jesus used the concepts of salvation and kingdom interchangeably. For example, when the disciples asked Jesus whether few would be saved, Jesus spoke of how many would "recline at table in the kingdom of God." Salvation is best understood as a kind of belonging. To be saved is to belong to and participate in the kingdom of God—a kingdom where Jesus is King (Christ). This is why in his itinerant ministry Jesus called people in the towns of Galilee to band together and live out the kingdom of God in assemblies he called "church." We should never forget that the church originated as Jesus' own idea. The church was not an optional addendum to the mission of Jesus, but the very heart of it!

The Christian life is not a solo project and it was never intended to be. Christianity is not primarily a set of privately held beliefs but a shared life. Nevertheless, the rise of Christianity as private pietism has obscured this truth. Much of the ethos in American Protestantism is sadly captured in the film The Apostle when the preacher played by Robert Duvall baptizes himself—an act of privatized spirituality that would have been utterly absurd in Apostolic Christianity, but is an accurate icon of Americanized Christianity. "I don't need the church, I'll just baptize myself." It's in the sense of salvation as a kind of belonging that the saying of the Desert Fathers is true: "One Christian is no Christian."

None of this critique of private spirituality is an attempt to paper over the glaring failures of the church. The failings and infidelities of the church are real and need to be acknowledged and repented of. But as disheartening as the failures of the church may be, they are nothing new. One of the strange truths about the church is that there has never been a golden age. Never. Not during Apostolic times, not during Early Christianity, not during Christendom, not during Medieval Christianity, not during the Reformation, not even during times of modern revival. No, there's never been a golden age, the church has always been plagued by problems because it has always been populated by sinners. And yet it survives and somehow gets on with its task of preserving and passing on the message of Jesus. So, if you have a personal relationship with Jesus, you can thank the church for making it possible. Without the church there is no sacred text, no sacred memory, no preserving of the faith, no passing on of the gospel, no knowledge of the life, death, and resurrection of Jesus Christ.

Though I'm honest about the persistent shortcomings of the church, I am not cynical. In the end I think Origen's ultimate defense of the church against the attacks of the pagan critic Celsus is still valid: "Come see our churches." Despite the fact that churches are comprised entirely of sinners, Jesus has never and will never divorce his bride. The church remains the most visible expression of the kingdom of Christ. You may say I'm a dreamer, but I'm not the only one, so let me just say it. There's no place on earth like the church. A place where Matthew 25 is just a normal day—a place where the poor are fed and clothed, the sick are helped and healed (who do you think invented hospitals?), a place where the immigrant is welcomed, and the prisoner is given dignity. A place where everyone is saint and sinner. A place where a judge and a felon can sit side by side on the same pew with equal status in Christ. A place where we not only carry each other's burdens, but when necessary carry each other, because, despite our vast differences in education and opportunity, opinions and politics, we are learning to love one another like Jesus loves us—unconditionally. Yes, I know I'm speaking like a dreamer, but I'm dreaming with my eyes wide open, because I've seen everything I've just described in churches all over the world.

This is why I love *Ordinary Church: A Long and Loving Look* by veteran pastor and keen thinker Joseph Beach. Joe has been writing this book for as long as I've known him. And that's why it's more than a book, it's really a love letter. Pastor Joe loves the church because he loves the church's Lord. Pastor Joe doesn't love the church as an abstract concept—love in the abstract is always cheap and easy—but as a pastor of one congregation for almost four decades. Decades-long pastoral longevity is something Joe Beach and I have in common—that and our fanatical obsession with the music of Bob Dylan. So, when Dylan sings, "'Come in,' she said, 'I'll give you shelter from the storm,'" we both instinctively think of the church. The church at its best is the compassionate bride of Christ who offers comfort and shelter to those "burned out from exhaustion, buried in the hail." I know this is true, because I see it in one way or the other every single Sunday.

Ordinary Church is an excellent book because it is both crisp and clear in its arguments, as well as kind and compassionate in its delivery. Joe Beach is too much of a pastor to merely offer theological critiques of the "I'm so done with church" sentiment. This book about the church (and clearly written with "dones" in mind), is written in a kindly, pastoral way. Ordinary Church is a pastor talking tenderly to people he loves about the church he loves. I sincerely wish that every pastor of a church, every Christian who loves the church, and especially every Christian who thinks they're done with the church would read this beautiful book.

> I've heard newborn babies wailin' like a mournin' dove
> And old men with broken teeth stranded without love
> Do I understand your question, man, is it hopeless and forlorn?
> "Come in," she said, "I'll give you shelter from the storm"

Brian Zahnd

Lead Pastor of Word of Life Church in St. Joseph, Missouri; author of *Water To Wine*

CHAPTER ONE

Introduction to the Ordinary Church

"When Hauerwas writes about the church, he seems to think of people who have brought the same casserole to every funeral luncheon for the last twenty-six years."

-William T. Cavanaugh

"Joe's gonna freak!" shouted a very precocious two year-old girl from the back seat of a car.

A few years ago, a good friend of ours was driving to church on a Sunday morning with her two-year-old daughter, Reagan, in the back seat. While driving, our friend received a call from her mother who needed them to come over right away. Reagan's Grandma had just lost her husband to Alzheimer's a few months before and was having a difficult morning. Our friend hung up her phone and said to her daughter, "well, Reagan, Grandma needs us. We can't go to church today." The little girl in the back seat responded immediately, "Joe's gonna freak!"

What kind of freak freaks out over someone missing church?

When I first heard that story I both laughed and cringed. I laughed because it's a cute story but I cringed because I didn't realize I was that obvious. I cringed because I didn't want to be *that guy* that "freaks out" about "church attendance" – *that guy* that passes out guilt-trips like they're going out of style. Or, if I am *that guy*, I, at least, want to be understood. This book is my attempt to explain myself. This book is the culmination of forty years spent in an ordinary church as an ordinary pastor – thinking, praying, speaking, and writing about the church.

To all those who think the "institution" of the church is not worth defending or saving, to all those who have been abused, misused, burned out, or just plain bored out of the church – I beg your patience. To all of you "post-church" friends, please give me a chance. I doubt this book (alone) can bring you back – but it can't hurt to listen to each other's stories. To all those who've never been interested in the church in the first place, I hope you catch a glimpse of the church's goodness and beauty. And, maybe most of all, to all those who claim Jesus as Lord, I pray that you'll be encouraged and challenged towards a more robust, loyal, grateful, and maybe even a more self-sacrificing participation in the body of Christ.

Just in case you already suspect that I might be a touch out-of-touch or judgmental, (based solely on a two-year-old's testimony), I really don't normally come across that way. You can ask anyone: I don't have a judgmental bone in my body – except when it comes to dispensationalists, hyper-Calvinists, picky eaters, and pushy drivers. Other than that, I'm usually the most accepting person on the block (I have proof from the Myers-Briggs). Seriously, though, I'm stressing this for a reason: I'm well aware that my experience does not necessarily fit everybody else. Each of us answers to the Lord, not to me, and I'm glad. I think I'm being honest when I say that my goal in this book is to somehow paint a picture of the church – the *actual* and *ordinary* local church - in such a way that might lead the reader to take a long and loving look at her – and maybe even see a glimpse of the extraordinary bride of Christ.

So, what is it that I have been trying to say about the church that has given people - even two-year-old children - the impression that I'd freak out if someone missed church? Well, in one way or another, I've been trying to say, that *to be a Christian is to be part of a Christian community - period – and that this is an essential part of what it means to follow Christ.* To put it more precisely:

To be a Christian is to be ***in Christ***
To be in Christ is be ***in the body of Christ***
To be in the body of Christ is to be ***in an actual ordinary church family***

You may wonder why I'm insisting on that word, "ordinary." Believe me, I'm fully aware that it's not an exciting description of a church. Just last week, for instance, a good friend of mine asked me: "are you sure you want to use that word? It's not very sexy. You do realize that it's a horrible title from a marketing standpoint, right?"

"Yes, I realize that," I replied. "That's sort of my point."

A couple of months ago, I was having breakfast with another friend of mine (who was a retired pastor) who had similar reservations. He was telling me all about the church growth seminars he'd recently attended (which I found odd since he's a manager of a Sherwin Williams paint store in Northern Michigan). He was also telling me about some recent Christian conferences and concerts and he could tell that, as usual, I wasn't overly impressed (he was right – he knows me well). He blurted out, "OK fine, Joe! You just stick with *us four and no more*! Go ahead and just keep doing maintenance on your little ol' church." My co-pastor was also with me at this breakfast and we both had a good laugh over this all-too-familiar sparring match. This retired pastor friend of mine (and paint store manager) has been going to these conferences and concerts his entire life. Here's the kicker: he has never liked a single church in his entire life that he has actually belonged to! And he's not alone. I've had other close friends over the years that have never been too thrilled by the churches they actually belonged to – choosing instead to get their thrills at conferences, concerts, revivals, and worship events *elsewhere*. Always *elsewhere*. It was always more spiritual and more exciting and more powerful - *somewhere else.* Anywhere than right here in this ordinary place.

I was reminded of a comment I had just read the day before. I was reading a gripping story by Kate Bowler in her book called "Everything Happens for a Reason: and other lies I've loved." Kate tells the story of receiving a diagnosis of Stage IV cancer and how she faced it with honesty and courage and how to best live with her husband and son and career, in light of her new normal. The reason I bring it up is because of her emphasis on living gratefully in the present. In the book, Kate confesses that she habitually commits the sin of not living fully in the present, in the everyday ordinariness of her life. She writes that her sin went deeper than just failure "to smell the roses." While I was reading her book, I kept thinking of our tendency to do the same with our families, our friendships, and our churches. She calls her sin "the sin of arrogance, of becoming impervious to life itself. I failed to love what was present and decided to love what was possible instead." She describes being always focused on *the next thing. There's always the next thing.* Finally, she confessed, "I must learn to live in ordinary time, but I don't know how." I read that section just a few days after my breakfast with my pastor friend so I immediately thought of the church and of this book I'm trying to write. I think we so often fail to love ordinary time and our ordinary lives and the actual ordinary church that's right in front of us. It's easy to succumb to the temptation to look ahead to the "next thing" or "the more exciting thing." I thank God for Kate Bowler and I pray for her and her family. She made me think about our lives and our churches. Her story made me want to say something similar about our relationship to the church:

We must take a long and loving look at our ordinary church.

THE CHURCH IS IN TROUBLE

I have a dream. My dream is that Christians in America would regain a commitment to their local church family. I realize that this isn't a major news flash but Christians in America don't seem to have a very high view of the church and its role in their Christian lives. At least when it comes to the ordinary *local* church, that is. I've seen some recent studies that debate this observation of mine, but it seems to me that regular "church attendance" - however boring that phrase may sound – is in decline. There may be exceptions to this in certain regions of the country and in certain segments of society, but there does seem to be a general decline in most American Christians' attachment to a particular "home church." I realize that many folks may still claim a home church – whether they attend regularly or not – but I'm referring to regular weekly attendance and regular participation in the life of the church. Many culprits receive blame: secularization, consumerism, hyper individualism, or the privatization of faith, just to name a few (not to mention the many failures of the church). Call it what you want but any way you slice it, I am one of those who believe that the Christian church throughout the western world is suffering from a weak or non-existent ecclesiology. That's the fancy way of saying: the church doesn't play an important role in the lives and thoughts of many self-professed Christians. It's a way of saying that many Christians aren't that committed or connected to their local congregation (their "home church") and I think it's killing us.

One of the main culprits may very well be the hyper-individualistic and privatized way we view the world in general – and the way we view spirituality/salvation in particular. In chapters five through eight, I take aim at these defective and destructive elements. Before that, in chapter two, I'll take a look at the state of the church in America. In chapter three, I attempt to demonstrate that the New Testament concept of church is an actual, official local congregation. After that, I'll tell my own story and that of my church. Finally, in the last few chapters, I'll discuss what an ordinary pastor of an ordinary church looks like (or should look like). This section is not just for pastors, though. It is for anyone interested in what the church is all about.

Speaking again of an overly individualized and privatized view of salvation, in chapter seven, I discuss an ancient religious shrine at a place called ***Eleusis*** (thanks to a New Testament scholar, Gerhard Lohfink, for this insight). ***Eleusis*** was a place where for a thousand years pilgrims in the ancient Roman empire would visit in order to obtain "personal salvation." I think we are living in a time and place that views salvation in eerily similar ways:

Salvation with "no strings attached.
Salvation with no social consequences.
Salvation without any necessary creeds or beliefs.
Salvation that's completely personal and private.

I contend that we American Christians are immersed in a similar kind of hyper-individualism and consumerism like we saw in ancient Eleusis. I contend that popular American spirituality could be called "Eleusis Revisited" or "Eleusis 2.0." It's what you hear regularly on T.V. and radio interviews and sermons, from pulpits around the nation, and from many of the bestselling "Christian books." It has seeped into the church and shaped our common faith and practice. Christianity in America, at the popular level, appears to me to be a baptized version of this same Eleusis-type spirituality. Eleusis 2.0 with a fish on it (and an American Flag, of course). I truly believe that this version of the faith is actually a rival religion. I believe that our view of salvation and our attachment to our home church are connected – and I believe that it is a matter of life and death. The church in America will live or die to the extent that the Christians in America are deeply embedded in local congregations throughout the land.

It is my assertion that a central and essential part of following Christ is regularly gathering together as his body, in his name, in a "home congregation," to worship Christ, proclaim him, pray to him, sing to him, to receive his body and blood in Holy Communion, to share his presence and power with one another, and to go *together through life*. Here's one way to describe my thesis:

There is more to the Christian faith and the Christian life
than going to church every week to worship God together,
but it is never less than that.

This book is my attempt to help restore and reaffirm the all-important central role of the local church in our lives together. I urge you to consider the possibility that participation in a covenant community is at the center of the Biblical story, the apostles' teaching and practice, and the church's life from the very beginning. I also urge you to consider that this simple truth is largely ignored by American Christians and is a major cause of the church's loss of identity, power, holiness, and mission. As difficult and old-fashioned as churchgoing may seem, I urge you to take a second look at it. Over four decades in my current church, this ordinary life in an ordinary church has developed into a passionate love affair with the local church. By this, I don't mean that I've liked everything about my church. Hardly! What I do mean is that all of my critiques and arguments qualify as a lovers' quarrel. In that sense, this book is also my love letter to the church – the regular, ordinary, local church.

Of course, to say "ordinary church" is like saying "ordinary family" which is like saying nothing. So, let me say it clearly: just as there are no ordinary people, there are, in fact, no ordinary churches. If you look closely enough, every church (like every person) is extraordinary. Nevertheless, I think that we all know what I mean. Just as we all know ordinary men and women that actually exist (in contrast to supermodels that don't) we all know of ordinary churches that actually exist. I'm referring to those churches that we actually belong to – the little church on the corner, the church in the small town, the church we grew up in, the ugly church in the declining urban part of town, the neighborhood church that lacks adequate parking, the storefront church that's still dreaming of someday moving to a nicer location, the church still renting at a school ten years after it stopped dreaming altogether. I'm also referring to new missional startups, underground churches, and old cathedrals. I'm not so much writing about the supermodel churches with the airbrushed pictures on T.V., in the magazines, or on the billboards. I realize that there are a few of those that seem to still exist – especially in what's left of the southern Bible Belt - but usually if you give them a decade or two – and take a close look at them from the inside out – you'll see that they, too, are ordinary. I'm referring to Catholic, Orthodox, and Protestant churches. I'm referring to non-denominational churches. I'm referring to regular, ordinary churches of all types, sizes, and flavors.

EUGENE PETERSON FOR DUMMIES

There's something else you need to know about this book. This book is a tribute to Eugene Peterson. You will notice from beginning to end that I unashamedly come from the *Eugene Peterson school of pastoral ministry*. This book is my thank you letter to "Pastor Pete," the "pastor to pastors." When I began writing this book Eugene Peterson was a young man. In his later years, I got to meet him and become friends. Recently, as I was finishing this book, he went on to his heavenly reward. I will forever miss him and will always cherish the exquisite gift of his friendship, the time I got to stay in his home on the banks of Flathead Lake in Montana, his encouraging letters and phone calls, and most of all, his (and Jan's) love to me and to all of us ordinary pastors in the world. When I told him that I was writing a book about the church and how he had taught me everything I knew, he wrote to me saying, "Yes, I very much would be pleased to be included in anything you write about the church and the pastoral vocation." That's all the encouragement I needed to hear from my hero.

I call Eugene Peterson the apostle to the ordinary pastor of the ordinary church. He has served as my reliable guide and mentor for nearly forty years. He has provided a lifeline to many of us down here in the local church trenches. Everything I write in this book about the local church has been shaped and flavored by Eugene's life work. His books, lectures, sermons, interviews, and even personal conversations inform every word I write. This book, therefore, is written from the perspective of a pastor and will reveal my heart about the relationship of a church to its pastors (and vice versa) but is not a book written solely for pastors. To me, Eugene Peterson's greatest gift to the church was recovering the dignity of the pastoral vocation and showing us the beauty and glory of the ordinary congregation. In one sense, this book is a summary of Eugene Peterson's insights and passions internalized and worked out in an actual congregation over several decades - one person's experience, application, and interpretation of Peterson's life work.

Over the years, as Eugene sat at his desk writing about the pastoral vocation and the local church, he was writing to me. I mean, specifically, to me. I told him that one day. I said, "Eugene, I was the absolute bulls-eye of your target audience. You were writing to me. Thousands of others were (thankfully) eavesdropping and benefitting greatly from your work. But you were writing to me. You can't get any more regular than me. And you can't get a more regular (or ordinary) church than mine. This is as regular as it gets. And that's all it will ever be." He said, as only Eugene can say it (that is, slowly, sincerely, and with a gravely voice) "well, Joe, that's a very kind thing to say." This was typical Eugene who, in person, was rarely wordy.

All of which brings me to repeat myself one more time: nobody is *actually* ordinary. No church family is *actually* ordinary. I know that. In a way, that's my main point. It's also a central theme in all of Eugene Peterson's writing and teaching ministry. Through everything he writes or speaks, he's attempting to provide us with new eyes – eyes to see the glory in the ordinary pastor, the ordinary church, the ordinary Christian, the ordinary person. In other words, if I was to give a title to Eugene's life work it would be: "*the glory of the ordinary*." He's saying that if you and I learn to take *a long and loving look* at ourselves and our churches, we'll begin to see them for what they actually are: Creations of the Holy Spirit, image-of-God souls in the making, and miracles that don't look much like miracles – very much like our Lord Jesus Christ when he was born as an ordinary human being in a very ordinary setting. *Oh, how we desperately need new eyes!* It's always been human nature to be unimpressed by the ordinary church - as unimpressed as humans were with the unimpressive way of Jesus.

My prayer is that the Holy Spirit might use this book to provide a few of us with new eyes to see the church as he sees her – and to see again our holy calling to participate in that ordinary local church.

ONE LAST WORD BEFORE WE BEGIN

As you read, remember two things: this is my story and the only story I know. I really don't "freak" if someone is walking a different path for different reasons through different seasons. Please believe me: everything I write is to be read through the lens of God's amazing grace. I don't judge you or anyone else. There are special situations in all of our lives which sometimes prevent us from finding a church home for a season. All I ask is that you consider (or re-consider) that there may be an ordinary church out there that needs you as much as you need it. I also ask you to consider the possibility that grandma was right all along: we really should go to church. Every Sunday. I know, I know, things have changed and our lives are overloaded with hectic chaotic stress. And yet, in spite of it all, I still believe that Grandma was more right than wrong and, for several years, I've wanted to write a book about that belief. This book is my attempt to do just that. My goal is to share the beauty and the glory that I have found in my own messed up regular church family - in hopes that others may still find reasons to show up.

This book is *not* a "how-to" book about church or pastoral ministry. I don't care too much for those kinds of books anyway. I think each pastor and each church is so unique that there is no one-size-fits-all approach. As Eugene Peterson often said, "The pastoral vocation is the most context-specific vocation in the world." This book is not a scholarly treatment on the nature of the church or on which church is the true church or anything of the sort. There are excellent books on those subjects (see the list at the end of the book). In that sense, my thesis that American Christians suffer from a low view of the church (i.e. a weak ecclesiology) applies equally to Roman Catholics, Eastern Orthodox believers, and Protestants. It applies to the high church and the low church. It applies to both large and small churches, to both urban and rural churches. I've often said to my Catholic theologian friends: "this lack of commitment to the local congregation - this low view of the local church - is not a Protestant problem or a Catholic problem. It's an *American* problem (hyper-individualism). Or, better yet, I guess you could say it's a *human* problem" (self-centeredness). Sadly, it's also a *systemic* problem. A growing percentage of the poorest among us, including the lower working class, are not attending church for a number of reasons – partly because churches in the decaying areas of society have either left or died. But, more on that in a moment. Okay, let's begin.

CHAPTER TWO

The State of the Union

"My dear Wormwood... Surely you know that if a man can't be cured of churchgoing, the next best thing is to send him all over the neighborhood looking for the church that 'suits' him..."

- C. S. LEWIS

The rise of the "Nones" and "Dones" is well known. On a regular basis, we hear reports that an increasing number of Americans check the "none" box when asked to give their religious affiliation. Apparently, among the younger generations, this is particularly true. It's also increasingly true of the "white working class" – a huge chunk of America that simply doesn't belong to any religion. The Pew Research Center refers to these as the "nothing in particulars." For some reason, this religiously unaffiliated demographic is disproportionately white, male, and uneducated.

We also hear of an increasing number of Christians who say they are "done" with "organized" religion or the "institutional" church (or the "traditional" church). These are those of the rapidly growing "ex-church" (or "post-church") movement. Another group of Christians still retain a vague sense that the church is important. They would even say that they, of course, "have" a church – but, in reality, they attend less and less frequently. Whether this is due to an ever-encroaching secularism, a power outage in the church, or just to the ever-increasing hectic, chaotic, overloaded nature of our lives, it seems that the church is in trouble. One observer wondered, "maybe it's the failure of the church – the Catholic church's abuse scandals, evangelical's politicization, mainliner's lukewarmness."

Whatever the causes, America is rapidly becoming more secular and less religious. And just in case you think these trends aren't necessarily negative, think again. Even though this book's focus is on my fellow Christians and our decreasing commitment to our local churches, allow me to focus on this side note just for a moment. Numerous top-shelf sociologists and political scientists, regardless of where they fall on the political spectrum, are saying the same thing: "The unchurching of America is at the root of America's economic and social problems." The argument goes like this: when the churches abandon the poorer sections of society (whether by "white flight" or by shutting down), it leads to the erosion of civil society which leads to the collapse of community which leads to the collapse of the family, which leads to death and despair throughout the land. Another way of putting it: what the poor and working class need most from the wealthy is not their money. It's their fellowship. It's community. It's eating and drinking the Lord's Supper together. It's wealthy people going *together through life* with poorer people – just like the Apostle Paul stressed to the Corinthians. My point for now is simply this: church attendance is on the decline and it's a life and death matter: for both the church and the world-at-large.

As mentioned earlier, declining church attendance is particularly true among the young. Several studies show that the church is losing its members from the "millennial" generation at an alarming and "unprecedented" rate. One millennial blogger, Sam Eaton, had this to say:

> *Turns out I identify more with Maria from The Sound of Music staring out the abbey window, longing to be free. It seems all-too-often our churches are actually causing more damage than good, and the statistics are showing a staggering number of millennials have taken note.... church attendance and impressions of the church are the lowest in recent history, and most drastic among millennials described as 22- to 35-year-olds.... As I sat in our large church's annual meeting last month, I looked around for anyone in my age bracket. It was a little like a Titanic search party...*

Hardly a day passes when I don't hear or read something about how church attendance is on the decline. Believe it or not, at least among Christians who like to read blogs, church attendance has been a hot topic for over a decade. Donald Miller, for instance, wrote a blog several years ago in which he shared some of his thoughts about his own church attendance. A firestorm immediately erupted in the blogosphere. Donald Miller is a well-known author, speaker, coach, and business leader who had become a New York Times bestselling author when he published his book, *Blue Like Jazz*, in 2003. Since then, he has written several additional books, produced movies, started some companies, and much more. To be fair, I should mention that I very much enjoy and appreciate his books. I've also heard him speak on several occasions and I respect him immensely for his work. In his books, speeches, and interviews (at least to me) he comes across as someone who loves the Lord, loves his wife, loves the people in his life, lives life to the fullest, and seems to respect pastors and the church in general.

Anyway, in this particular blog (about not connecting to God through traditional worship services in either the singing or the sermons), and in a follow up blog (and podcast interviews), Donald Miller shared some of his thoughts about the church. He wrote about education theory and learning styles and how all of this might relate to his struggle to connect at church on any meaningful level. He wondered if some of his struggle to connect or relate could be a result of his having a different learning style (than the church's traditional "academic lecture" format). He also mentioned that he doesn't experience genuine community while sitting in rows with two hundred people all facing forward listening to a lecture. So, he finally concluded that regular church attendance was not a wise use of his time. At the time he wrote his explosive blog, he had gone five years without attending church with any kind of regularity. He also mentioned that he's not alone. That's the statement that started the firestorm:

Most of the influential Christian leaders I know (who are not pastors) do not attend church.

As you can imagine, Donald Miller received quite a backlash from several of his readers. He said later that he was actually surprised by how negative and, especially, how personal the backlash was. He later admitted that when he wrote the initial blog, he was fairly naive about how sensitive an issue this was. He also admitted that had he known that his remarks would traumatize so many people he probably wouldn't have published his thoughts. Nevertheless, he did publish them and they ignited an important conversation. In my opinion, much of the criticism he received was unfair or, at least, misdirected. People accused him of narcissism and of being anti-church. I don't think either is true. I think he was just being honest about his life and how he was experiencing Jesus and community.

I wished, of course, that Donald Miller remained part of a "congregation" for the reasons I will give in this book (or, that he finds his way home to an actual church in the future - if he's not in one already), but I do think he made several good points. First, he does see the value of having committed relationships in his life and to being accountable to a handful of close and trusted friends. Second, I agree with him when he cautions us about using language like "biblical church" or a "biblical model" of church. Quite often, when we describe something as "biblical," we mean "my opinion about the Bible." When we criticize Don Miller or anyone else for dropping out of regular traditional church, let us never assume for a moment that the typical modern church that they left behind is anything close to a "biblical" model of church. Miller wrote:

> *Today, many churches look like night clubs complete with pastors being piped in on video. It's quite brilliant and I've no problem with it, it's just not my thing. I don't like night clubs. And I don't like lectures and I don't emote to worship music. And I still love Jesus. It's shocking, but it's true. That said, let's stop using the word "Biblical" as some sort of ace card when it comes to how church should be done.*

In Miller's blog, I found some of his words to be very affirming of our own church. Here's a good example:

> *In fact, I'd argue that by making the church smaller, less formal, less organized, less institutionalized and more like the chaos of a family structure, the church would be moving more toward the historical church in Acts and less like a culture-formed institution...*

Those words warmed my heart because if my church is anything it's smaller, more informal, less organized, and more chaotic than most churches. When I read those descriptions of the church I was thinking, "me… me…… me... me..." (mimicking Bill Murray's character in the movie, *Groundhog Day)*. Donald Miller was describing our regular messed up church, and hundreds of other ordinary churches all over the world, and it was affirming.

One criticism of Donald Miller's blog came from another Miller: *Kevin* Miller of Christianity Today. In CT's online Leadership Journal, Kevin responded to Donald's blog about dropping out of regular church attendance with an article of his own entitled, *The Strange Yet Familiar Tale of Brian, Rob, and Don*. This title was prefaced with "Wings of Wax?" and subtitled, "A decade ago, they stood as the leading voices of our evangelical future. We all know what happened since. But do we know why?" I should note that Kevin Miller soon removed his post with the following comment:

> *I still stand by my fundamental point in this article, namely, that we need a movement-wide, soul-searching look at the results of our ecclesiology. However, the article has produced a food fight in the church's cafeteria that I did not intend. I regret that it has not been helpful to the body of Christ.*

I thought to myself: *How are we supposed to have a hearty discussion about the importance of regular church attendance if everyone keeps apologizing and removing their posts?!* It should be obvious by now that I would agree with Kevin about us needing to work on our ecclesiology. I do think, however, that he picked the wrong fight with the wrong people - and received some valid criticism by lumping them all together. The three targets of his article, Brian McLaren, Rob Bell, and Don Miller, are each their own person and are at quite different places in life and ministry. Donald Miller, for instance, never claimed to be a pastor or a theologian. He is a thoughtful writer and a creative thinker - who happens to be a follower of Christ. Rob Bell was a gifted pastor, he is an insightful teacher, and a talented speaker. He resigned from his church and is doing other things out in California. He may or may not be worthy of Kevin's criticism of being a "church drop-out." Brian McLaren, however, seemed to be unfairly included with the others, at least when it comes to regular church attendance. I, for one, was thankful for McLaren's response on his own blog:

> *Should spending 24 years as a church planter and pastor qualify one as a quitter? Although I did leave the pastorate 8 years ago, I didn't in any way leave the church. I'm a quiet and grateful member of a congregation in the community where I now live. My years as a pastor make me deeply grateful for every sermon, song, prayer, and Eucharist that I am privileged to share in when I am at my home congregation.*

I applaud Brian McLaren's commitment to his "home congregation." That phrase warms my heart because I think (for reasons I explain in the next chapter) that is exactly what is meant by "church" in the New Testament and in the ancient church. All in all, I am glad that people are passionately discussing and debating this hot topic. I wish Kevin Miller had focused only on Donald Miller's comments about church attendance because, in the end, I think Kevin had a great point. In fact, I think his main point was, and is, extremely important. In many ways, it is the main point of this book. I'll put it in bold and capital letters so you can't miss it:

"WE NEED A LOFTIER ECCLESIOLOGY"

Here's how Kevin Miller went on to explain:

> *It turns out that we evangelicals need a loftier ecclesiology, where the words of St. Cyprian sound*

> *natural to our ears: "He can no longer have God for his Father who has not the Church for his mother; . . . he who gathers elsewhere than in the Church scatters the Church of Christ." Are we willing to grow in our love for Holy Church? To accept her teachings, her worship, her cultural rejection? Will we embrace not just the Head but the Body, and love not just the Groom but the Bride?*

Rachel Held Evans is another writer who, in recent years, waded into the treacherous waters of this discussion with her delightful book, *Searching For Sunday: Loving, Leaving, and Finding the Church.*

> *[Sadly and tragically, as this book was in the publication process, Rachel passed away. Thousands of us were shocked and heart-broken by the sudden loss of this young wife and mother. Rachel was kind, thoughtful, and respectful. As Becky Castle Miller wrote, Rachel loved God and loved people, and many people credit her for saving their faith, others thanked her for literally saving their lives. I thank God for Rachel and pray for her husband, children, family, and friends.]*

As always, Rachel's writing was beautiful, honest, and soul-searching. Her book thrilled me, fascinated me, and frustrated me - all at the same time. Upon finishing it, though, I was more in love with the church than when I began. She painted a picture that made the church seem both beautiful and significant. I loved how she structured the book around the sacraments because she believes that it was the Holy Spirit-empowered sacraments that actually brought her home to the body of Christ. In the end, she concluded, "all we have is this church - this lousy, screwed-up, glorious church - which by God's grace, is enough." Rachel writes that it was the sacraments that actually drew her back to the church after she had given up on it. She writes,

> *...the tangible, tactile nature of the sacraments invited me to touch, smell, taste, hear, and see God in the stuff of everyday life again. They got God out of my head and into my hands. They reminded me that Christianity isn't meant to simply be believed; it's meant to be lived, shared, eaten, spoken, and enacted in the presence of other people. They reminded me that, try as I may, I can't be a Christian on my own. I need a community. I need the church.*

Of course, for Rachel to find her way back to the church, she first had to leave the church. She dropped out for a while and went through several years of disenchantment and disillusionment with the church. After growing up in a fairly standard Protestant evangelical church, she began to grow increasingly disenchanted and disillusioned with what she perceived as evangelicalism's many repugnant characteristics:

hyper-certainty, arrogance, partisan politics (usually right wing), a hyper-literal biblicism, militarism, nationalism, a particular position on women in ministry, a strict theory on the atonement, a certain theory on inerrancy, and many more. Just so you know, I'm sympathetic to her negative reaction to these stereotypical characteristics of the evangelical subculture and I share her distaste for most, if not all, of these. Several times while I was reading her book, I found myself wanting to assure Rachel that there are tens of thousands of us out here that are equally turned off by these "isms" that plague our evangelical world. At one point, I even wrote in the margin of the book: "Rachel, your problem isn't with the church; it's with the evangelical sub-culture's version of the church." Another time I wrote, "Your problem isn't the church. Your problem is the Americanized version of the church: the watered down, thin, shallow, individualist, consumerist, easy-cheesy-cotton-candy version of the church!" Fortunately, she found out soon enough that there was an entirely different way to express the Christian faith: the more historical, robust view that has always been part of *The Great Tradition.* She discovered the good stuff: scholars like N.T. Wright, Scot McKnight, and many others who helped her to see the grand scope of the gospel, salvation, and the kingdom - that had been there all along.

Like many of my friends, Rachel did not ultimately *leave* the church, she *found* the church. She rediscovered the real thing. She left the watered-down Kool-Aid version of Christianity and began to discover the deep rich wine of The Great Tradition - a church with deep roots, ancient practices, stunning beauty, and time-tested creeds. She was re-captured by a more historically rich liturgical worship. In a speech entitled, "Keep the Church Weird," Rachel reported that she is frequently asked, "how can we keep young people in the church?" After her years of "searching for Sunday," reconnecting with the church, and thinking deeply about the church, she reached this conclusion:

> *We already know the answer to that question [of how to keep young people in the church]. And, contrary to popular belief, it's not about making the church more hip. It's not about adding coffee shops in the lobby and fog machines on the stage. It's not about pastors who wear skinny jeans... It's about communion. It's about baptism. It's about confession. It's about healing. It's about death and resurrection and all the beautiful weird things the church has always been doing.*

Amen, Rachel! Amen! I was so glad to hear her articulate what so many of us have been feeling. I am not only glad for Rachel's conclusion; I am glad for her search. I was fascinated by Rachel's journey away from the church and then back again. As I said, I very much appreciated her honest, beautiful writing. A couple of my friends read her book at the same time I did and we all had very similar reactions to it. We were glad we read the book. We all remarked that the book both encouraged us at times and made us cringe at other times. The cringing came only because we knew how difficult it was to stay home (in the church) while she went on a journey - even though we shared most of Rachel's critiques of our evangelical sub-culture. Staying wasn't easy but stay we did. And we were still there when Rachel and others like her returned. For now, though, I just want to thank God for both Rachel Held Evans and for Donald Miller and for others like them who are making us rethink everything we think about the church.

This discussion (about church attendance and the traditional church) has actually been a hot topic for many years now. Seven years ago, for instance, I wrote a blog on this subject. In that piece, I mentioned that a good friend of mine had dropped out of traditional church. This friend of mine is a man I deeply respect - he's a thoughtful Christian with a PhD in philosophy – but he just dropped out (of any kind of "institutional" or "traditional" church). We had many discussions and I struggled to understand his heart. He, like many others, thought that it would be better to simply be a follower of Christ outside of official "organized" churches. He said that he meets with close friends in various settings and that he is committed to a group of fellow disciples who meet in various contexts and that he feels it is "enough." In other words, he does not consider himself a "drop out" from church. He truly believes that he has "dropped in" to the real thing. He believes that his small community of like-minded friends constitutes "church" for him. In the next chapter, I will discuss this all-important question of what constitutes a church. About the same time as my friend dropped out, there were several voices in print and in the blogosphere promoting this line of thinking. Frank Viola, for instance, and the late, great "Internet Monk" (Michael Spencer) have written books in support of moving away from this idea of having a "home congregation" in any traditional sense. Anne Rice, the famous author turned Christian, said that she was also dropping out. She said, "I'm remaining a follower of Christ - but leaving the church. I love Christ - but can no longer handle the company of his disciples."

Another man I respect, Wayne Jacobson, a former pastor in my hometown of Visalia, California, has dedicated much of his life and ministry to these "anti-institutional" ideas and "post-church" sentiments. He and his partner are the guys who helped first publish the book, *The Shack*, (which went on to sell millions of copies and eventually became a major motion picture). Like me, Wayne grew up among the orange trees and grape vineyards of central California. And, like me, Wayne became a pastor of an ordinary (wonderful) church. Eventually, however, he decided that the cultural definition of a pastor no longer fit him. I don't think it fits me either, to tell you the truth. But unlike me, Wayne left the institutional church behind. He continues to write insightful and provocative articles and books about the amazing love of God.

Speaking of *The Shack*, I'm one of those people who very much enjoyed that book and have often recommended it to folks struggling to understand how God can be a good, loving, and gracious God in the midst of unthinkable tragedy and suffering. I think it's a helpful book on several other levels as well - especially in its dramatic portrayal of God as being an eternal triune dance of interpersonal and radical love. As far as I can tell, the book beautifully accomplished its purposes (as did the movie, which, by the way, was very well done - in my humble opinion). I thank God for the author, William Paul Young. His grace, humility, and kindness come through loud and clear in his writing, speaking, and to all who have had the privilege of meeting him (as I have on numerous occasions – but Paul McCartney once told me to never name drop, so I don't). I'm only bringing up *The Shack* book because of its apparently low view of the significance of the local church – and how nobody seemed to notice or care about that. I know that wasn't Paul Young's purpose or focus so I'm not really critiquing him or his book. My point is this: most people in our society have such a low view of the church that few people even noticed or cared about this missing element in the book. (Those who critiqued it did so on other grounds – *unfairly* in my opinion). Or to put it differently, many American Christians were far more likely to notice (and be offended by) the fact that God the Father was represented in the book by an African-American woman than they were to notice the absence of the local church in Mac's re-emerging spirituality. Likewise, I heard many people complain about a hint of universalism in the book but I heard nobody complain about an absence of an ecclesiology in the book. But, again, I only bring this up as an illustration of *the state of the union* in America. I have no interest in critiquing *The Shack* or its wonderful author.

SO, WHAT IS THE STATE OF THE UNION?

As you may have guessed by now, the thesis of this book is that we American Christians need a more robust ecclesiology (i.e. a higher view of the local church). In that sense, I am never fond of any sentiments or movements that seem to minimize a Christian's commitment to a particular local church. I can understand slogans such as "I love Jesus but not the church" (which is the Christian version of "I'm spiritual but not religious") but ultimately, I find them sad at best, and lacking courage at worst. George Barna put out a book several years ago charting this ex-church phenomenon and called it a "revolution." Keven Miller, in his critique of Barna's book, said that a better word for this movement was "abdication." I tend to agree with Miller. He wrote, "Barna's enthusiasm for the *First Church of the Individual* raises troubling questions." To my mind, that would be an understatement. Scot McKnight made a similar observation and critique:

> *George Barna did that study about "radical" Christians who had very little commitment to their local churches.*

> *He saw them as "white hot Christians." I don't know how someone could be a "white hot Christian" and not be committed to a local church. God's design in this world is to build his people through the body of Christ that takes place in local communities, in local churches.*

As I hope to show in the next chapter, I believe that there is a fundamental difference between congregation and friendship. I think this distinction is often lost in our world today - maybe especially by younger Christians (i.e. the famous "millennials"). As McKnight puts it:

> *I would say that when young people say that they value "community" what they really value is "friendship." Community is a fellowship of "differents." Many times, what is referred to as community is actually a fellowship of the "sames." ... Community is building relationships across generations and with people who are sometimes like us and sometimes not like us... with people who we may or may not even like. But we are drawn together as the body of Christ.*

Alissa Wilkinson said it this way:

> *Our Christian subculture is marked by church hopping. We stay put as long as it suits us, until we are offended or decide we're not being "fed." So, wanting to quietly*

> *validate our own identities, we tend to silo ourselves into churches where everyone looks like us, talks like us, likes the same movies, and won't embarrass us in public. But what if we took a cue from popular culture's push for diversity and realized that surrounding ourselves with our duplicates only makes us more self-centered?*

A well-known recent book at the center of this discussion is called *The Benedict Option* by Rod Dreher. The book has gained a wide and appreciative readership and an equal amount of passionate critique. Many people think that its assessment of our current situation exaggerates how dire things are (which seems like a valid critique to me). Others find Dreher's suggested solutions lacking in places. One of Dreher's main appeals, however, seems absolutely spot on and of vital importance. He states over and over the absolute important place of a local home congregation. This emphasis is consistent with the thrust of this book. Here's a collection of a few of his statements:

> *We have to return to the roots of our faith, both in thought and practice... in short, we are going to have to be the church..., centering our lives on the church community... The church can't just be the place you go on Sundays - it must become the center of your life. We would have to choose to make a decisive leap into a truly countercultural way of living Christianity, or we*

would doom our children and our children's children to assimilation.

To that, I say "amen!" A thousand AMENS!

YE WHO ARE WEARY COME HOME

Ultimately, as much as I appreciate and respect my brothers and sisters who simply can't stomach the regular, ordinary church, I have the following questions. In other words, these would be my questions to anyone thinking of leaving the "ordinary" church or to those who are planning to stay away indefinitely. Please take these as honest questions to ponder and discuss – rather than accusations or judgments:

- *What if the Holy Spirit has called you into a congregation of "differents" and placed you into a body that desperately needs you?*

- *What if it's not all about you and your comfort? What if you are part of a congregation because that is your family - that loves you and needs you? What if you are there to worship God and to help others do the same?*

- *What if we grow best by working out our offenses, frustrations, and boredoms - learning to practice love, acceptance, patience, and forgiveness? What if the church's purpose in our life is more to make us holy than to make us happy?*

- *Does it worry you that it's difficult to pass on the faith to your children without institutional and relational habits, practices, and rituals? In other words, would you agree that it's hard to pass on a purely individualized spiritual feeling to our children?*

- *Who will keep the lights on so that the church is there for you when you feel the urge to drop in or to return with your children?*

- *Do you have people in your life to whom you are accountable (for your loyalty, commitment, growth in holiness, etc.)? Does it bother you that without a home church it's easy to be self-centered and unaccountable to a community of people who need you? Is it easy, for instance, to avoid people different than you?*

- *Admitting that the typical (regular, ordinary) American church has many blind spots and problems (over-programmed, over-leveraged, over-stressed, overly focused on survival and maintenance, and on and on and on), what if you are called to be part of the answer and part of the solution and part of the needed change?*

I would add a few more questions and comments directed to those who have left the church – either temporarily or for good. Most of these have arisen out of my own church context:

- *Who will keep these churches open so that you can go when you decide that you feel like it, when you feel that you need the inspiration and spiritual boost that a church service can provide?*

- *Who will volunteer for children's ministry, clean the buildings, pay the electric bills and the salaries of the pastors?*

- *Who is going to keep the food bank full and serve the hungry all week?*

- *Who's going to love on the children of this neighborhood and mentor them as they grow up?*

- *Who's going to sit with the single mother as their boy friend lies dead in the street outside?*

- *Where are you going to have grandpa's funeral and who's going to organize and run the service and pre pare the family dinner afterwards?*

- *Who's going to dedicate and baptize your children?*

- *Who's going to sit by the river all day and talk your son out of killing himself? (Yes this has happened).*

- *Who is going to prepare, sanctify, and serve the body and blood of Christ, week by week, year after year?*

- *Who is going to teach your children the story of Christ when you feel like dropping in?*

- *Who's going to take kids up to summer camp every single year for fifty years - kids that can't afford to go anywhere else?*

In the end, I must admit, there are times when the "I love Jesus but not the church" crowd feels and sounds like individualism pure and simple. Jonathan Leeman, for instance, put it well in his response to some of the post-church blogs:

> *Your idea of community, to my ears, honestly, sounds more American and Romantic (as in the -ism of the 19th century) than biblical. All authority remains with the individual to pick and choose, come and go, owing some of the obligations of love, perhaps, but always on one's own terms, happy to stay as long as the experience "completes me" and my sense of self.*

Before we move on, I need to add some words I wrote several years ago in a published blog on this subject: I'm not saying that the critique that comes from the anti-institutional church movement isn't valid. The reasons for dropping out are often legitimate and real. Churches, especially the ones that I've encountered in the North American evangelical sub-culture, are often awash in all kinds of assumptions, blind spots, and ways of doing business that are in great need of reform. I'm not saying that local churches never hurt or harm people or groups of people. I'm not saying that churches shouldn't do everything possible to avoid the superficiality and trivialization of worship that is all too common. I'm not saying that we should endorse the depersonalized, functionalized, market-driven approach so prevalent in many of our churches.

What I *am* saying is that even with all of that valid critique, we, like Jesus and his first followers, should think long and hard before walking out on the local church to which the Holy Spirit appointed us. To me, most of the New Testament's instructions about elders and deacons, Baptism and Holy Communion, singing together, elders who work hard at teaching and preaching, "coming together as a church," and all the "one anothers" (loving, forgiving, accepting, welcoming, encouraging, rebuking, etc.) make no sense in the so-called revolutionary "post-church" world. Returning to Kevin Miller's critique of the book, *Revolution*:

> *Want to become a revolutionary? Here's my counsel. Trade your copy of Revolution for Life Together, the manifesto written by Dietrich Bonhoeffer in the dark days of Nazi Germany. Then, to do heroic and revolutionary exploits, stay committed to your local church – something 20 million people no longer have the courage to do.*

Please allow me to enlarge on that challenge. In fact, let me preach my guts out for just a moment or two: Do you want to do something revolutionary and radical and rebellious? **Go to church.** Yes, you heard me right. If you want to do something truly courageous and rebellious in a secular culture, do something *religious*. I dare you. I double dog dare you. That's light years more revolutionary than getting a tattoo or sleeping in on a Sunday morning or hanging out with a few like-minded friends. That takes ten times more courage than it does to sit outside the church and criticize "organized religion." Commit yourself to a local community of fellow believers, make yourself accountable to them, serve Christ, and serve your fellow believers with loyal love for years (or decades). Now there's something truly non-conformist! If all you do is declare that you are "spiritual but not religious" or that you "love Jesus but not the church," then you are doing nothing more than being a boring conformist. You are nothing more than an echo of the pop culture surrounding you. You are doing nothing more than walking lockstep with the crowd. I'm not saying that everyone who repeats those slogans is insincere or shallow.

What I am saying is that those are not radical or rebellious thoughts – not in the least! They are the thoughts of the cultural mainstream these days. If you want to be a true rebel, stand up to "the man," and go against the system - *go to church, pray the prayers, sing the songs, practice the ancient habits and disciplines, and commit yourself to a community consisting of your brothers and sisters in the faith* – brothers and sisters totally unlike you in almost every way. Now that would take some guts and would freak out everyone around you. One more way to say it: *everyone is religious... so stop saying you're not!* Everyone is practicing the rituals and beliefs of some religion, even if your religion is the pop culture religion of secular America, so no more nonsense about you not being religious. After all, we all know that *you gotta serve somebody*… and you're serving somebody… you just might not realize it.

My hopeful prayer is that God would grant us that kind of courage. I pray that American Christians would increasingly do the courageous and revolutionary thing: stay together long enough to create a multi-generational family that would make it possible for our children and our children's children to be Christian. Stay together long enough to provide a multi-generational community - loving one another, serving one another, and learning from one another. Sounds like the New Testament, doesn't it? Sounds like something that the gospel births and sustains. Sounds like something that preserves the gospel, proclaims the gospel, teaches the gospel and, then, lives out the gospel. In this sense, the ordinary congregation truly is something extraordinary - a peculiar people, God's precious possession, the bride of Christ - and constitutes God's main project in the world today.

If you want to read one person's courageous return home to the ordinary church, read Sarah Bessey's beautiful journey called *Out of Sorts*. In her book, Sarah shares her "there and back again" journey of growing up in an ordinary church and leaving and eventually making her way back home again. I don't mean to make light of her journey out of the church. Her pain seemed genuine. Her disappointment seemed absolutely sincere. I encourage you to read her story. Eventually, she reports that she came home and that *home* to her was the regular everyday ordinary church – much like the one she grew up in. I love her sentence,

"I practiced the radical spiritual art of staying put."

She realized that, in the end, she believed in messy imperfect structures after all. She believed in teaching Sunday School and helping with youth lock-ins. She believed in "just checking on you" phone calls. She believed in showing up for weddings and funerals and in bringing enchiladas to new mothers. She discovered that she even believes in the frustratingly slow-to-change structures and long slow consensus-building required of elder boards and deacon committees. She writes that "this is not work for the faint of heart." And finally, she wants what many of us want. She wants her children to grow up with the imperfect community of God just like she did, writing, "*I want my tinies to know what my voice sounds like when I sing 'Amazing Grace.'*"

May Sarah's tribe increase. In my book, she is the true non-conformist radical revolutionary of our day. Please don't misunderstand. I'm not saying that I got the impression that she's trying to be some kind of radical. Not in the least. I'm saying that I get the impression that she's simply "at home" with Jesus, her husband, her children, and the family of brothers and sisters that the Holy Spirit has graciously provided. And to me, in light of the state of the union in modern America, that's as counter-cultural as it gets.

CHAPTER THREE

The Church in the Church's Scripture

"Common worship... is the sine qua non of being a Christian. Any other way of honoring God is, in both Testaments, simply unthinkable."

- Fleming Rutledge

In one of his last sermons, Karl Barth said something like this: "I wish Martin Luther's wish had come true and that in our creeds and confessions, we had used the word *congregation* instead of *church*." In other words, Karl Barth wished that when we confess our beliefs, we would confess, "I believe in the congregation," to which I say, "Amen! A thousand amens!" I wish that Barth's wish that Luther's wish had come true! The word *congregation* speaks of an actual community of believers who share life together and, thus, it would serve as a constant reminder in our creeds that the church universal is inextricably, organically, and spiritually linked to actual congregations around the world. The church, in fact, exists in no other form.

In other words, most of us have no problem saying that we believe in the church. It's the congregation that we're not so sure about. Virtually all Christians, including American Christians, confess belief in the church. Christians, worldwide, for two thousand years, regularly confess:

I believe in the holy catholic Church,
the communion of saints.

Our confession, however, is not our problem. Our problem, in my opinion, is a widespread and pervasive misunderstanding of what the church is and its essential role in Christian life and practice. This confession of belief in the church might be the most difficult part of the creed - especially if we include the idea of an actual congregation when we think about the church. I often wonder: it may take more faith to believe that the ordinary congregation is God's divinely ordained plan (and the body of Christ) than it does to believe in the Deity of Christ.

I believe that this widespread and pervasive misunderstanding comes from our defective view of what it means to be a Christian. When we define the Christian life in merely individualistic terms (or solely in private and personal terms), our participation in a local church inevitably becomes just one important (voluntary) option among many others. In other words, we all know that church is important in some sense.

But we also assume (in our current cultural assumptions) that we are free to attend (or not) and that we are free to participate (or not) according to our desires, schedules, tastes, feelings, energy levels, etc. To view church in any other way would feel like "legalism, pressure, guilt, and law" - all things that are anathema in our culture. I think Stanley Hauerwas articulates this core problem and hits the nail on the head:

> *One of the great problems of Evangelical life in America is evangelicals think that they have a [personal] relationship with God that they then go to church to express - but church is a secondary phenomenon to their personal relationship and I think that's to get it exactly backwards! The Christian faith is mediated faith. It only comes through the witness of others as embodied in the church.... So, evangelicals, I'm afraid, often times... make the church a secondary phenomenon to their assumed faith and I think that's making it very hard to maintain disciplined congregations.*

I hope we grasp his point. Hauerwas is saying that when we begin with our individualistic faith and our *personal relationship with our personal savior* (a phrase not found in the Scriptures), and when that is the central defining nature of our Christian life, we will inevitably view church in a vague universal way - as some large invisible "kingdom-like" entity to which we sort of belong. We will inevitably view local congregations as optional, voluntary associations of like-minded people who come together to express their individual faith relationship with God - *if and when they want to, if and when they choose to, if and when it fits their schedule.* Hauerwas goes on to say that when we do this, we "fail to realize that without the church we would have no Jesus." He means that it is the church who gives us Jesus, who first witnessed to the risen Christ and preserved the story of Jesus. It was the church who gave us the Bible in the first place. It is the church who baptizes us into Jesus, who feeds us Jesus in the Lord's Supper, who nourishes our faith in Jesus on a regular basis. It is the church who encourages us along the Jesus Way. That is the reason, Hauerwas says, that he has no problem with that old (uncomfortable) phrase, "*No salvation outside the church.*" Don't tell anyone, but I don't either.

SO, WHAT IS A CHURCH?

As we begin to think about the church (and actual congregations) we are immediately confronted with several key questions - the first of which is the million-dollar question:

- ***What constitutes a church?***

- *Can't we just get together regularly with a group of Christians - close friends to whom we are committed and with whom we have communion, prayer, worship, discussion, etc., and with whom we go through life together?*

- *Are we required to go to a formal meeting place and meet in that particular place every week?*

- *Do we have to worship on Sunday? Every Sunday? Should we make people feel guilty if they don't attend regularly?*

- *Can't we participate in more than one church? If we are getting what we need, spiritually, from several different sources, isn't that the important thing?*

I have received these questions from people over the years. Here's a typical response:

> *"My church is made up of close friends with whom I hang out. My church is made up of small groups that I belong to that meet for prayer and open discussion. Who's to say that this isn't "church" for me? I can also get plenty of good teaching and enjoy great praise music any time of the day anywhere I want. Who are you to tell me that this isn't "church" for me? I get a lot more out of these relationships and resources than I ever got out of a traditional church. Who's to say what constitutes a real church, anyway? Isn't is ultimately about my relationship*

with Jesus and how I treat people and how I live my life?"

These responses and questions, of course, will inevitably bring us to the Bible. What does the Bible say about all this? This question actually makes me nervous because, even though I hold a high view of Scripture, I have grown weary of how so many of us evangelical types use (and misuse) the Bible. I have no interest in playing what I call the "Verses Game." You know the game: "*my verses versus your verses*" until someone wins. I have no interest in providing a bunch of "proof texts" to prove to you that there is one clear "biblical model" of church in the Bible (Spoiler alert: there isn't one). *However* (and you knew a *however* was coming), I'm going to attempt to make the case - from Scripture - for the vital centrality of an actual congregation in the life of a Christian. I want to show that when the Bible speaks about the church it often (usually) has an actual congregation in mind. So, I am asking you to think with me about *the church in the church's scripture*.

Obviously, I am not going to deal with all of the relevant texts. I could make the connection, for instance, between the Sabbath principle - *Honor the Sabbath* - and the New Testament church's observance of it – and the reasons behind the early transfer to the Lord's Day. I realize that most Christians, and certainly most pastors, are familiar with the relevant passages in the New Testament that refer to the church. Most of us, for instance, are well aware of how the first Christians met regularly (daily in some cases but, for sure, every Lords' Day) and that they "devoted themselves to the apostles' teaching and to the fellowship, the breaking of bread and to the prayers" (Acts. 2:42). We are also familiar with the command in Hebrews: "not forsaking the assembling of ourselves together, as is the manner of some" (Heb. 10:25). We are also reminded of the words of Jesus "I am the vine; you are the branches. If you remain in me and I in you, you will bear much fruit; apart from me you can do nothing" (John 15:5). Or when Christ so identifies himself with the church he says to Saul, the persecutor of the church, "why are you persecuting me?" (Acts 9:4). Or when he commands us to "eat his body and drink his blood" (John 6:54). Jesus is emphasizing that the church is more than a voluntary association or a religious organization. The church is his living body – a living organism. We find our life in the church because we find Jesus in the church, his body.

What I want us to focus on, however, is one particular idea that comes through in the words and behaviors of the apostles and the first Christians. That idea is this:

There was (in Paul's mind and in the mind of his readers) some obvious and commonly understood definition of what constituted a church.

I hope to establish this idea – from Paul's first letter to the

Corinthians, in particular. Before we look at that passage, I need to state what I believe about the bigger picture of the Bible. I want us to see how our hyper-individualism has led us to often miss the obvious: that the Bible, to a large extent, is the story of God's people - or the story of God's attempt to form a people of his own (for the sake of blessing the whole world). For the purposes of this book, then, I do believe that the church (the actual local church - and our loyal participation in it) is at the center of the Jesus story, the gospel. I do believe that at the center of the grand epic narrative of Holy Scripture is the story of God's People, his holy covenant community - and of our participation in it. The story of Jesus, in other words, includes the story of Israel and the Church. I want to assert that church is part of the gospel (or, at the very least, its immediate fruit and implication). The good news is the Royal Announcement of the crucified Messiah, the Risen Lord Jesus Christ, his resurrection vindicating and validating his death on the cross for the forgiveness of sins - *and* as the fulfillment of the Israel story and Israel's intended expansion and extension into an international church. As Trevor Wax puts it: the gospel is a three-legged stool: it makes an announcement, it tells a story, and it births the church.

I hope also to demonstrate that salvation is a kind of "belonging." I think that after centuries of an overemphasis on the "corporate" or the "collective" aspect of human society, the pendulum swung to the other extreme of hyper-individualism.

For most of the last century or so, American culture and, therefore, the American church, has suffered from this overemphasis on the individual. Many of the church's current woes and weaknesses are the result of this malady. In fact, our distinctive articulation of the gospel has been so distorted (mainly diminished) by this hyper-individualism that it's lost much of its power. Thankfully, at least from my perspective, the Holy Spirit is leading the church through a mid-course correction - and using the recent work of N.T. Wright, Scot McKnight, and many others, to help us regain a "full gospel" again - a gospel as grand as it was always intended to be - a gospel rightly focused on Jesus Christ and his kingdom - and a gospel that includes both the corporate and the personal.

In many cases, *we reduced the gospel down to a personal plan of post-mortem salvation and a formulaic ticket to heaven.* I praise God that we are awakening from our "enlightened" slumber and are working to restore the true gospel of the King and his Kingdom. We easily forget, however, that something else was reduced when the gospel was reduced - and that "something else" was our view of the church. And we are not hearing as much about this great loss. Of all the adventures in missing the point, one of the most destructive is our common de-valuing of regular committed participation in an actual congregation. This book is my attempt to shed some light on this forgotten subject and restore "going to church" to its rightful place in our pursuit of Jesus Christ and his kingdom.

Or, if you prefer me to put it a bit more theologically, I hope this book helps a few of us restore our commitment to common/gathered worship and going *together through life* as part of an actual ordinary congregation.

BUT, WHAT DOES THE BIBLE SAY?

Ok, it's time for some Bible and Theology. I will be brief but please do put on your thinking caps for a few minutes. One Sunday, a few years ago, I was prepared to preach on my favorite subject (yep, you guessed it: Jesus Christ and his church! The sermon was basically a condensed version of this book). Well, a day or so before the sermon, a missionary couple that we support came into town and mentioned that they'd be attending our Sunday morning service. Believe it or not, I preached my sermon instead of having our friends preach! (Don't worry, I heard about it afterwards). The missionary couple happened to be our friends, Steve and Dawn Bryan, and they graciously encouraged me to go ahead with my sermon plan, which I did. They, of course, did speak for a while, too, and gave a report on their life and ministry in Ethiopia. (They have since moved to Chicago to teach at Trinity Evangelical Divinity School). After the service we met for Mexican food on Federal Boulevard - which is always a special treat for us locals. Anyway, here's the good part: Steve, a New Testament scholar (PhD, Cambridge), said that he appreciated my message and then asked me if I had ever read Peter O'Brien's article on the church (in IVP's *Dictionary of Paul and His Letters).* I couldn't remember if I had so he suggested that I read (or re-read) O'Brien's article. He thought it would affirm much of what I was saying. I did read it – and I am glad I did. My suggestion is that everybody give it a careful reading.

In the article, O'Brien confirmed much of what I'd been thinking about the meaning of the word "church" (*ekklesia*) in the New Testament. Every detail that I include below is chosen for a reason. Each sentence is part of the biblical and theological foundation of this entire book, so please read carefully – even if you think you already know this stuff. You can, of course, reach your own conclusions after reading his article, but here is how I would summarize Dr. O'Brien's findings:

- In the centuries before the New Testament, the term *ekklesia* was used for political gatherings, the assembly of "full citizens" of the *polis.* In other words, *Ekklesia* only existed when it actually assembled. In the LXX (the Septuagint, the Greek translation of the Hebrew Bible), *ekklesia never* referred to Israel as a national unit. It always referred to an actual assembly or gathering of people. "It did *not* designate an 'organization' or 'society.'"

- *Ekklesia* is used 114 times in the New Testament – 62 times by Paul. Paul does not use the term as a *metaphor*. To Paul, it is descriptive of an actual object. Unless on the rare occasion when he uses the term for the "heavenly" church (i.e. the "future" church, the heavenly kingdom of God on earth), he only applies the term *ekklesia* to an actual gathering of people. *The primary use of the word ekklesia as a gathering of actual people predominates overwhelmingly in the NT.*

- The local church (each local church) is not *part* of the church of God nor *a* church of God. Each local church is *the* church of God – the only form it takes in this present age. Each local church is a reflection and manifestation of the "future *ekklesia*" (the completed, fulfilled Kingdom on earth – which will, indeed, be a universal gathering when the whole universe becomes the dwelling place of God, the holy of holies). The church (each local church) truly is an outpost or a colony "from the future" – that is, each church is an *eschatological* church, the kingdom *in advance* and *in locale.*

- Christians were reminded and admonished (Heb. 10:25) to assemble in local congregations here on earth, for this was an important way in which their fellowship with Christ was expressed. When they met like this with each other, they also met with Christ himself who indwelt them corporately and individually.

Well, that's my interpretive summary of O'Brien's excellent article. As I said, others may read it and reach their own conclusions. Earlier, I mentioned Karl Barth's comment about the word *congregation.* In that same sermon, Barth made the same point as O'Brien. He said that *Ekklesia* certainly means congregation, a *coming together*. Barth then said,

> *It is best not to apply the idea of invisibility to the Church; we are all inclined to slip away into... a sort of Cloud-cuckooland, in which the Christians are united inwardly and invisibly, while the visible church is devalued. In the Apostles Creed it is not an invisible structure which is intended but a quite visible coming together... When I say congregation, I am thinking primarily of the concrete form of the congregation in a particular place.... The Christian congregation arises and exists... as a divine 'convocatio' - those called together by the work of the Holy Spirit assemble at the summons of their King.*

THE CRUX OF THE BISCUIT

This brings us to my primary text. As we mountain climbers would put it, this passage is, for me, the "crux of the biscuit." I may be placing too much weight on this one section of

Paul's letters, but at least give me a fair hearing. I want us to take a close look at Paul's discussion of Holy Communion (in 1 Corinthians 11). I'm particularly interested in Paul's six references to the Corinthian Christians *gathering together as a church*, and I'd like to quickly list them and then explain what I mean. The passage is 1 Cor. 11:17-34. Here are Paul's references to the "congregating" Corinthians:

1. ***"your <u>meetings</u>" (11:17)***
2. ***"when you <u>come together</u> as a church" (11:18)***
3. ***"so then, when you <u>come together</u>" (11:20)***
4. ***"<u>the church</u> of God" (11:22)***
5. ***"so then, brothers and sisters, when you <u>gather</u>" (11:33)***
6. ***"when you <u>meet together</u>" (11:34)***

Here's the kicker: Paul seems to assume that his readers know exactly what he's referring to when he refers to their official meetings and their official "gathering togethers," if you will. Please hear me well: It seems to me that Paul is talking about an actual, recognizable, definable, regular, official gathering of an actual congregation. You could say that those words constitute the beginning of my answer to the question, *what constitutes a church?* I'm saying that whatever a church is, it is - at the very least - among other things - something that is:

Actual, recognizable, definable, regular, and official

Especially when you consider that the Apostle Paul contrasts these official *public* gatherings with *private* ones: "Don't you have *homes* to eat and drink in?" (v. 22). I take this to mean that *in private* (i.e. at home, at the coffee shop, at the pub, on the river, on the golf course, etc.), we can eat and drink what we want (within reason) with the people we want. We can do anything (morally acceptable) with anyone we choose. When we hang out with our chosen friends, we may even pray together and discuss Christ and our faith. We may share our burdens and our struggles and minister to each other's needs in deeply personal and meaningful ways. All of that is wonderfully precious and significant. In fact, I hope we would all be so lucky as to have close friends in our lives with whom we can share all of life - the good, the bad, and the ugly - including our faith. But that's different than *gathering as a church*. When we *gather as a church,* we are to accept everyone, wait for everyone, welcome everyone, include everyone, and, if possible, reconcile with everyone – especially those most unlike us. As Scot McKnight puts it, church is a "Fellowship of *Differents*" not a "Fellowship of *Sames*."

The Apostle Paul is clearly making a distinction between *friendship* and *church*. When we gather as a church we are to eat and drink together *as a congregation*, as a family of God, as the unified body of Christ, an actual local church (young, old, rich, poor, black, white, left-wing and right-wing, educated or not…). Yes, I think there is more to being a church than this.

For now, though, I am simply saying that a church is something identifiable and definable and that it is distinguishable from hanging out with close, like-minded Christian friends.

Now, one could make the argument that this passage in 1 Corinthians 11 is not discussing anything like what we mean by a modern Sunday morning worship service. It is true that Paul is discussing what was most likely an evening meal shared by the believers - a "Lord's Supper" that may have begun with breaking bread together and ended with the sharing of the cup. It may very well have been something akin to our "potluck" dinners in that people may have brought food to either eat themselves or to share with others. This could be the meaning of Paul's rebuke, i.e. that the rich were eating a lot of good food and drinking good wine while the poor were stuck with little or no food and wine - or at best poor food and poor wine. I believe, however, that the point remains. If this eucharistic practice was at the heart of their common meetings then there was still something distinguishable between these meetings and their private ones. There remains something distinctive and recognizable and official about their church gatherings. So, my main point remains: *one of the main elements that constitutes a church is this welcoming of people most unlike ourselves***.** This is the point made by Philip Yancey, in his classic column, "Why I Don't Go to a Megachurch:"

> *I resist the trend toward megachurches, preferring small-*

er places out of the spotlight. I never understood why until I came across this paradoxical observation in G.K. Chesterton's Heretics: "The man who lives in a small community lives in a much larger world... The reason is obvious. In a large community we can choose our companions. In a small community our companions are chosen for us." Precisely! Given a choice, I tend to hang out with folks like me: people who have college degrees, drink only Starbucks dark roast coffee, listen to classical music, and buy their cars based on EPA gas mileage ratings. Yet, after a short while I get bored with people like me. Smaller groups (and smaller churches) force me to rub shoulders with everybody else.

Henri Nouwen defines "community" as the place where the person you least want to live with always lives. Often, we surround ourselves with the people we most want to live with, thus forming a club or a clique, not a community. Anyone can form a club; it takes grace, shared vision, and hard work to form a community.

Corinth is not the only New Testament church in which it is assumed that the believers regularly gathered in some kind of identifiable congregation. Most of the New Testament's descriptions and instructions regarding the Christian life would be unintelligible outside of regular, loyal, long term participation in a local congregation. For instance, the idea of singing and praying together, loving and forgiving one another, accepting and waiting for one another, rebuking and challenging one another, and all the other "one anothers," simply make no sense outside of a congregation going *together through life*. Love, acceptance, and forgiveness usually (and only) mean something within the context of shared time and commitment. In other words, we have to share life together close enough and long enough to truly hurt and offend one another enough to require real forgiveness. We have to spend enough quality time with each other to truly experience enough annoying, irritating differences to make acceptance genuinely meaningful.

Another important distinction to make is this: *the church is more than just a voluntary association of like-minded individuals*. In modern American society, this is a radically counter-cultural statement. As Hauerwas pointed out in the quote above, the typical American evangelical Christian simply assumes that a Christian is someone who has a personal relationship with Jesus who may or may not choose to express that faith in a church. Church, to many of us, is a *secondary, optional, voluntary* phenomenon in our Christian lives. Hauerwas says that this is exactly backwards! A Christian is someone who has encountered and received the witness of the church: Jesus Christ crucified and risen. In other words, the Christian faith has been mediated to them by and through the church. They *then* personally trust in Christ - yes! - but it is in the context of joining that very community of witnesses. That's why I like to say that salvation is a kind of belonging, a kind of joining. To be saved is to be placed into the covenant community of God. To say yes to Christ is to say yes to his friends. To say yes to the King is to say yes to his Kingdom. To say yes to the Father is to say yes to his family. To be a Christian is to follow Christ into his body, as part of his body. To say yes to Jesus' call to follow him is to take a step in his direction, or to take a step *with* him, and the moment you take that step with him you simultaneously take it with others. You simultaneously join others in the Jesus Way. I will focus on this theme in Chapter Seven, "The First Church of the Individual."

Here's another way to put it: a church is a fellowship of "differents" that is created by the Holy Spirit (to use Scot McKnight's term again). This is probably a bit controversial, but I do believe that the Holy Spirit places us into local congregations and forms us together into a family. I believe that a local congregation is a Holy Spirit created miracle into which we are placed and over which are placed divinely chosen servant leaders. I don't think it's merely a voluntary (or accidental) association of individuals who choose to attend when and if it fits them. It's a Holy Spirit created family with servant leaders chosen by God - pastors/elders shepherding an actual "flock" of which the Holy Spirit has made them overseers (Acts. 20:28), the actual "flock" that is under their care" (I Peter 5:2). Having said that, I realize that this can get very messy - as every congregation has imperfect pastors and imperfect members and it doesn't always work out so well in practice. But I still believe that we ought to at least consider viewing our church family as a divine appointment into a divinely created community.

One more thought: I mentioned earlier that there are always exceptions and extenuating circumstances to this "ideal" that I am espousing. I am reminded that there are Christians who have jobs or careers or family situations that prevent them from being in one place for very long. I'm also reminded that there are Christian communities in some countries who have to remain underground and maybe even mobile. I recognize and respect these circumstances. Again, my passionate convictions are directed mostly at typical North American Christians who aren't prevented from a committed and loyal participation in a local church home.

SO, WHAT COUNTS AS CHURCH?

As I said, I think the church is a recognizable, official, actual congregation of people *not* of our choosing and often most *unlike* us. You could expand on this and talk about the necessary servant leadership and the presence of baptism and the Lord's Supper. In the previous chapter, in our discussion of Donald Miller's blogs on church attendance, I quoted Jonathan Leeman. He had this to say about this question of what constitutes a church:

> *In other words, Don, the main thing I want to highlight in response to both of your posts is the difference between what you call "community" and what the Bible calls the "church." Jesus actually gave authority to those local assemblies called churches (Matt. 16:13-20; 18:15-20). The assembly is not just a fellowship, but an accountability fellowship. It's not just a group of believers at the park; it preaches the gospel and possesses the keys of the kingdom for binding and loosing through the ordinances. It declares who does and does not belong to the kingdom. It exercises oversight. And exercising such affirmation and oversight meaningfully means gathering regularly and getting involved in one another's lives.*

Amen!! So, my answer to what constitutes a church would be that the church is something actual and official, governed by official and recognized servant leaders, open to anyone and everyone the Lord calls, a fellowship of "differents," that proclaims the gospel, and administers the sacraments/ordinances.

CHAPTER FOUR

Amazing Grace Church

"The only thing I want in life is to be known for loving Christ, to build his church, to love his bride..."

- Kari Jobe

Here's something I've heard all my life: "The church is not a building. It's people." I've also heard this one: "you don't *go* to church. You *are* the church." I'm no longer so sure about these statements. I think that's another influence from Eugene Peterson. In his book, "The Jesus Way," Peterson questions this "anti-building, anti-institutional" mindset - which is common in our current culture. His words are timely, prophetic, and counter-cultural:

It is interesting to note that Jesus, who in abridged form is quite popular with the non-church crowd, was not anti-institutional... Those who followed Jesus, followed him into buildings, into religious institutions... We sometimes say, thoughtlessly I think, that the church is not a building. It's people. I'm not so sure. Synagogues and temples, cathedrals, chapels, and storefront meeting halls provide continuity in place and community for Jesus to work his will among his people. A place, a building, collects stories and develops associations that give local depth and breadth and continuity to our experience of following Jesus. We must not try to be more spiritual than Jesus in this business. Following Jesus means following him into sacred buildings that have a lot of sinners in them, some of them very conspicuous sinners. Jesus doesn't seem to mind... A spirituality that has no institutional structure or support very soon becomes self-indulgent and one-generational.

A place, a building, collects stories.

What a beautiful sentence. In my case, it rings true. I am a witness to the truth and beauty of that phrase. Our church has collected story after story. Six generations of stories! And those stories do indeed provide local depth and breadth and continuity. I've seen it in my life and in the lives of my children and my children's children. We all sense that our story somehow fits into the stories of our parents, grandparents, great-grandparents, and so forth.

I will never forget my wife's story of seeing her great-grandfather pass away during the Thursday evening service at Amazing Grace Church. She was only four and a half years old, but she's never forgotten that evening. Her great-grandfather was living with her grandparents (Pastor Kindschy's parents). Grandma recalled later that great-grandpa was unusually focused that evening – cleaning his room more than usual, staring at the house for a long time as they pulled away in the car. During the service, during testimony time, great-grandpa Lebsack started to give his testimony. He was too weak to stand so he spoke from his chair where he was sitting next to my wife's three-year-old sister, Sharon. He began speaking about God's faithfulness and how God always provides another generation that will preserve the faith and pass it on to the next. He said, "whenever someone dies, God in his faithfulness always raises up another leader. There was Abraham, Isaac, Jacob, Joseph, Moses, Joshua, David…" He went on and on, listing them all. Finally, he said, "And then in the New Testament, there was…" and he just slumped over and died.

Now, sixty years later, I know I am standing on holy ground as I watch my children's children playing around in that exact spot where their great, great, great-grandfather died – that spot where a child's *dad's mom's dad's mom's dad* passed away testifying to God's faithful provision. It was almost like a prophecy of God's promise to protect and guide us through the years. Six generations traveling *together through life* as part of a local church family. Collecting stories all the way.

And that's just one family. I could tell similar stories about many other family clans in our church. In the end, these stories being collected all belong to one family: our church family, the family of God.

The passion that drives the writing of this book is the passion to pass on a church to my children's children. As my friend Brian Zahnd likes to put it,

> *If our Christian faith is merely a "personal, spiritual" experience - without a deep commitment to the church and its practices - our children might be Christian but our children's children will not be.*

Or, to repeat Peterson's words, "A spirituality that has no institutional structure... soon becomes self-indulgent and one-generational." It is interesting that in many cases the most vocal among the I-love-Jesus-but-not-the-church folks do not have children. Or, at least, not yet. It's quite common for young parents to suddenly regain an interest in passing on the faith to their children and they instinctively sense that it's difficult to pass on an inner spiritual feeling (if that's all your faith is). The only way to pass on a "faith" to our children's children is to (among other things) raise them in the habits, practices, rituals, and beliefs of that faith - all shared within the context of a church family - and a life that reflects that all of those things are of central importance. Even if those rituals and creeds seem like the lifeless bark on a tree, let us never forget that without that strong protective outer shell, the tree would have no inner life whatsoever. The same can be said of an ugly lifeless skeleton. But without those bones - those strong protective structures – there can be no health or life in a body. Let him who has ears to hear, hear.

THIS CHURCH REALLY IS *AMAZING*

I have been "going to church" all my life. I had to. At first, my mother made me go. Then, for the last thirty years, my congregation made me go. They're one of these congregations that expect their pastor to show up every week. Well, it's time to give you a picture of Amazing Grace Church. As I've said, it's as ordinary as it gets. I have been a part of Amazing Grace Church in the southwest metro area of Denver, Colorado, for nearly forty years. Amazing Grace is a regular, non-denominational, multi-generational church. I still remember the first time I walked into a Sunday morning service during my freshman year of college. But let me first give you the back story.

I have only been part of two churches in my entire life! Before coming to Denver to attend college on a ski racing scholarship, I grew up as part of a church in a small farm town of central California. As you can see, my story is that of spending decades in an ordinary local church. I've spent the past thirty years (plus) as a preacher, teacher, and pastor in an ordinary church. Understandably (and conveniently) my theology matches my life experience and vice versa. I think that's typical - although I also hope that my theology of the local church is consistent with the biblical story. Nevertheless, this is my story and the passions and convictions that have formed over the years. I guess it's my way of saying: "I need to tell you where I sit before I tell you where I stand." Like Timothy, my faith in Christ was passed down to me from my grandmother and my mother.

> *"I am reminded of your sincere faith,*
> *which first lived in your grandmother Lois*
> *and in your mother Eunice and,*
> *I am persuaded, now lives in you."*
> - II Timothy 1:5

All my life, I've heard the statement that "God has no grandchildren." I understood that to mean that each person must trust God on their own (or, if you prefer, believe in God, surrender to God, or follow Christ – on their own). I took it to mean that they must personally respond in faith to the call of God. I understand this reminder but I think we can easily forget that the Christian faith is an *inherited* faith - or at least a *mediated* faith that is given to us by the church and, often, handed down to us by our parents and grandparents. We *receive* a faith that has been preserved through the ages and passed down through the generations and finally entrusted to us. Yes, I am called to personally surrender and personally trust and therefore, hopefully, personally experience the faith. But I don't get to make it up. We don't come to the Christian faith in a vacuum. The first witnesses of the resurrected Christ passed on that testimony to witnesses who passed it on to the next generation - right down to us in our day. In my case, it came from my mother and her mother and her mother.

My maternal grandmother, Irma Humason, was the matriarch of faith for our entire clan. She led us all with a firm faith in God. And I can say, without a doubt, she laid the foundation for my theology of the local church and my personal philosophy of ministry. Let me explain. You see, my grandmother was a lifelong Baptist. She grew up in a sophisticated family in Dallas, Texas. She and her family were core members of the famous First Baptist Church of Dallas (Rev. Truett and then, later, D.A. Criswell. I have no comment on the current pastor). My grandmother has the distinct honor of being the first woman to ever drive an automobile in Dallas. Her other claim to fame was that she (claims) to be related to the well-known Civil War (Confederate) general, Joseph E. Johnston (her maiden name). My cousin, Randy, is the family historian and has not found proof of this assertion as of yet. Either way, supposedly, my mother named me Joseph in his memory.

In the 1930's, Irma and her husband Guerdon Humason moved

to a small farming community in Central California's San Joaquin Valley named Orange Cove. It was there in those orange groves that my mother and father were raised and where I spent my childhood. I was baptized as a baby in the First Presbyterian Church of Orange Cove, California. Yes, you read that right: *Presbyterian.* My grandmother, a life-long committed Baptist, faithfully participated in the Presbyterian church for the next *seventy* years! The reason? There wasn't a Baptist church in town so she went to the nearest church and became part of that family until her passing at the age of 105 years. I grew up with her, living with her off and on over the years, studying the Bible, praying, and wondering together what God might have in mind for my life. I was deeply impressed by how she passionately followed Christ as part of a church family - through thick and thin. The church, for example, went through good years and bad years, good pastors and bad ones, conservative pastors and liberal ones, good choir directors and bad ones, dry times and revivals, and on and on for over seventy years. Through it all, my grandmother was unfazed. She followed Christ as part of this multi-generational congregation, no matter what, until I finally officiated her funeral in that same church. I saw firsthand, the beauty of a life lived in loyal love to God and to the brothers and sisters given to her. I personally saw the fruit of a faithful life lived within one single community of faith, for better or worse, through good times and bad times, "come hell or high water," and I've never gotten her saintly life-giving example out of my system.

When I was five, my own parents moved to a small farming community a few miles down the road called Exeter. This was where I grew up. We lived two houses down from the First Baptist Church and the church parsonage. It didn't take my mother long to return us to her family's Baptist roots. Before you get the wrong idea, you need to know that these Baptists were the nice kind of Baptists. They were the gracious kind. I didn't even know until years later that there was such a thing as mean-spirited, narrow, judgmental Baptists. When I arrived in Denver as an adult, I would often describe myself as a Baptist. My friends would say, "No you're not! Don't say that!" I didn't realize that to many of my friends, the only Baptist they'd ever met was the hateful narrow kind. The Baptist church of my youth, however, was located in what we would now call a "very evangelical" district of the American Baptists.

Until I started missing church because of my year-round ski racing career, I attended this ordinary grace-filled Baptist church every Sunday for Sunday School and church, every week for Youth Group, and every summer for Vacation Bible School. I attended Summer Camp as well and, like any good Baptist kid, went into the woods after one of those Summer Camp chapels and surrendered my life to Christ. My mother was the Sunday School Superintendent so we never had to wonder if we were going to church or not. I have a clear and fond memory of my Junior High Sunday School class. The class was taught by the Pastor in his study and had only two young people in the class: myself and some cute girl whose name I've long since forgotten. To this day, I remember the personal attention I received from the pastor as we read and discussed the scriptures together. There's a good chance that that little class with two members in it had a defining influence in my life. I will never forget the day when that dear pastor looked at me during one of our discussions and said, "Joe, you will probably be a pastor someday."

Those words stuck with me the rest of my life but they also caused me to be careful with my words! You never want to be the cause of some boy or girl spending the rest of their life barking up the wrong vocational tree. Whether my calling to the ministry came from God or from some pastor in a tiny middle school Sunday School class, or a combination of both, we'll never know. A call to gospel ministry is a mysterious thing. I've always loved how Fred Craddock, one of the greatest preachers of the 20th Century, says that he's not absolutely sure if he was indeed called or not. He says that, in the end, he doesn't really care. He's convinced that something needed to be said and that he knew what needed to be said, so he said it. Called or not, no harm was done. He's fond of quoting from an old hymn and then changing the last line:

I ask no dream, no prophet ecstasies,
No sudden rending of the veil of clay,
No angel visitant, no opening skies;
... just something to say.

Years later, when I was heading towards seminary and gospel ministry, many of my old friends and ski racing buddies seemed quite shocked by my chosen vocation. Knowing only the crude and rude ski racer, they just never saw this coming. They had no way of knowing that a pastor of an ordinary church had planted a seed in my heart years before. That small Sunday School class and the personal attention of the pastor shaped my philosophy of ministry to this day. It's one of the reasons why I don't mind small classes. It's one of the reasons why I loved it when my children were in a small class and got such close loving attention from their teacher. It's one of the reasons why I've always established and maintained close personal relationships with every middle school student that grows up in our church. And it's one of the reasons why I was so offended and enraged by the recent reckless and careless remarks of a well-known pastor who said that every Christian parent needed to find a church that had a huge middle school youth group (more on that in chapter six).

After I'd left home to pursue a full-time ski racing career, I heard that my dear pastor who had changed my life with his loving and attentive encouragement had moved to another church in another town - and had sadly taken his own life. My mother called me and told me that he'd made some mistakes or had some weaknesses and that he couldn't get past his own shame and that he'd committed suicide. My heart broke for him and his family. It's another reason why I'm so sensitive about the fact that pastors are first human beings who need friendship and support and forgiveness (more on that in chapter eight).

Anyway, when I turned 21, I continued to ski race but I decided that it was time to get some college in while racing at the same time. College racing seemed to make the most sense so I moved to Denver, Colorado, to attend school. I was actually a few months away from beginning college at Montana State University in Bozeman, Montana, but through a miraculous and bizarre turn of events, my life took a major and life-defining turn towards Denver. I've told this "miracle story" often but I may as well tell it again.

As I said, I had accepted an invitation to ski race for the Montana State ski team and was already accepted into the college. I fully expected to begin school at MSU in early September. One afternoon, however, early in the summer, I was driving my first car, my prize possession, a 1973 Green Ford Pinto station wagon with my buddy Steve Howard in the car as we drove through a little mountain village called Shaver Lake, California. He was living there at the time so he asked me to stop at the tiny Post Office so he could pick up his mail. He went in to the post office while I waited in the car. My dad and I had both lived in this little village in years past, at different times so, when I got tired of waiting for Steve to come out, I decided to go into the post office too. I thought I'd ask if there was any mail still sitting around under "general delivery" for either myself or my dad. I wasn't expecting anything, I just asked the question totally on a whim. I was just being the smart-alecky kid that I was at twenty years of age. I pushed open the door and shouted, "got any general delivery mail for Beach?"

A minute later, the postman said, "just a couple pieces of junk mail for Stan Beach," and handed me a couple of envelopes addressed to my dad. I glanced at them and one of them was a brochure that caught my eye because a picture of a ski racer was on the front. I could tell just by a glance that the skier in the picture was obviously a lousy racer but it caught my eye nonetheless. I think I vaguely picked up on the fact that the brochure was from some unknown little college in Colorado but it didn't seem interesting or relevant to me so I tossed it into the back of my car. Now mind you: to truly understand the magnitude of this genuine miracle you have to understand what I mean by the back of my car. I had long since kept the back seat down flat so I could transport my six pairs of skis and all the rest of my equipment, my five tennis rackets, most of my clothing and shoes, coats, other personal belongings, and my little tape deck along with hundreds of music cassettes containing the recorded albums of Bob Dylan, Neil Young, and the Rolling Stones. On top of that, I would toss every single bit of trash that ever entered the car. I'm not proud of this - but I'm not exaggerating one bit to say that this pile of possessions and trash - including hundreds of empty beer cans and coffee cups - was at least 30 inches deep from the driver's seat all the way back to the back of the station wagon.

Anyway, a few weeks later I was looking for something through the back window of the station wagon and that same brochure from the little college in Denver caught my eye again. I had forgotten about it but it had somehow recycled to the top of the pile again. I remember returning it to the bottom of the pile and forgetting all about it. A couple of weeks later, I had the same experience as this same brochure floated up to the top of the pile again and caught my eye. A third time I threw it into the pile and forgot about it. Finally, in July, it floated up again and once again caught my attention. This time I actually took the brochure with me into the condo where I was living with my dad up at Huntington Lake, California (which was about twenty-five miles further up the mountain from the little post office where this miracle story all began). I think I was finally irritated enough by this brochure's unwillingness to leave me alone that I sat down and took a look at it. It was from a little college called Rockmont College (which would later change its name to Colorado Christian University). This brochure mentioned that Rockmont College was a Christian college with a fairly serious ski racing team. I was a little bit intrigued. The Christian part didn't totally scare me off (like you might have expected) because I considered myself a life-long Christian and had been raised in the church and in the faith. For whatever reason, I filled out the form and mailed it off.

Several weeks passed and by early August I had honestly forgotten all about the pesky little brochure. One evening I was in the condo all alone and watching over the place (my dad was the manager of the entire complex and he was out of town) when the phone rang. I picked it up and discovered that it was the ski coach from Rockmont. He seemed extremely interested in recruiting me to the college and to the ski team. I told him that I was planning on leaving in a few weeks for Bozeman, Montana. He apologized for responding so slowly to my inquiry and said that he'd been out of the country for a few weeks. He promptly offered me a full scholarship including all tuition, fees, books, expenses, and even complete room and board. He then offered six pairs of skis and all other necessary equipment. I told him that I would need to continue racing on the regional and national circuits (outside of and in addition to the university events) while in school - and he immediately promised to cover all of those expenses as well. Finally, he promised that the ski racing team was part of Division One NCAA and that I could participate in the NCAA National Championships, if I qualified. I was a bit blown away by all of his offers and promises. I found out later that he was "creatively embellishing" some things – like the part about the Division One thing and that he actually had no authority to promise me most of the things he promised me. I think he was just overly excited – but I didn't know any of that at the time.

My dad came home the next day and I said to him, "you know, I got the weirdest call last night from a ski coach in Denver from a little Christian college called "Rockmont College" and he promised me the moon if I came there. Do you think I should even consider it?" My dad was a little blown away by it all too - but eventually, for many different reasons, I accepted the offer and made plans to head to Denver. Looking back forty years later, I stand utterly amazed over the fact that that moment radically defined the rest of my adult life, the lives of hundreds of others, and the lives of my children and their children for generations to come. I can't believe that the bizarre change of events that led to that last minute decision, stemming from that pesky little brochure, picked up totally on a whim in another village that I didn't even live in at the time, and thrown into my deep trash pile three separate times, and based on a set of extreme exaggerations from an overly excited ski coach during one late night phone call that I happened to take... would affect so many lives for so many years. The main reason I'm sharing this story is that it greatly affects my view of the local church. For whatever reason, for better or for worse, like it or not, it seems that God wanted me and my church together. I'm not sure if the church needed me or if I needed the church or a little bit of both. All I know for sure is that it took a miracle to put us together. It may not be a miracle on the level of the parting of the Red Sea, but if you knew me in 1978 and if you knew my green Pinto, it was close.

When I arrived at that little college, I discovered over the next two years that the ski coach had lied and overstated things beyond his authority. He was a good man, I think, but just overly enthusiastic about making his fledgling ski race program successful. To the school's credit, the president of the school at the time, a wonderful saint named Dr. Beckman, honored every single one of the coach's promises. I found out that I was the only actual ski racer on the team. There was a guy on our team - who became a good friend of mine, who actually was an Olympic Ski Racer. That was somewhat misleading, however, in that he actually couldn't ski very well (at least not compared to the serious racers I'd spent my life around) but had created the Costa Rica Ski Team (of which he was the only member) and had actually competed in several Olympics. He was the ski racing equivalent of the Jamaican Bobsled team, if you catch my drift. Naturally, though, the folks at the college didn't know anything about ski racing so they spent a lot of time and energy promoting their "Olympic Ski Racer" from Costa Rica. I didn't really care too much because I was too busy actually ski racing. For two years, I raced all over the country and also for the college, totally at the college's expense. Dr. Beckman finally had to inform me that the school was dropping the ski program and that they couldn't afford to support me any longer. Fortunately, I'd had the best years of my racing career during those two years and the University of Denver offered me a full scholarship to race for them so I promptly transferred to D.U. where I finished my ski racing career and from which I eventually graduated.

When I first walked onto the campus of that small evangelical liberal arts college, I experienced such radical culture shock I almost dropped out during the first week. In my youthful arrogance, I thought that I was just plain too cool. I thought I was too worldly wise for such a backwater nerdy place as Rockmont College in the late 70's. After all, I had just spent the last seven years in Europe and Argentina and New England and all over the United States from Mammoth Mountain, California to Aspen, Colorado, to Sugarloaf, Maine, travelling from resort to resort by private plane - and I was just *too cool for school.* The first year at Rockmont, I actually lived on the campus of Denver University with my ski racing buddies. So, after a night of partying with the D.U. students, I would drive my forest green Ford Pinto (with the uber-cool *Rossignol*-tinted banner across the front windshield) over to the Rockmont campus and walk into an evangelical subculture I knew absolutely nothing about. I tried to hide the can of Copenhagen in my back pocket and the hangover I was experiencing while trying to pretend that I understood the lectures on Deutero-Isaiah, the authorship of Ephesians, and the dispensational gap between Daniel's sixty-ninth and seventieth weeks.

On a side note, the Bible teacher dumping all of that new and confusing information on me was a man called "Coach Lindgren." Coach became one of my all-time heroes. He was a tall handsome man with deep convictions and deep integrity. He became a larger-than-life figure in my early years of re-commitment to the Christian faith: part John-the-Baptist and part Robert Redford. The first few weeks of my freshman year in college, during the all-school student retreat at Glen Eyrie, I met him and his daughter Katherine (probably the cutest six-year old girl in the universe). I was immediately in awe of Coach Lindgren. He was confident to the point of intimidating. Over the years, we became dear friends and I came to know his wife and five wonderful children. Tragically, Coach died of cancer at an early age. I will always love and cherish his role in my life. The sad and ironic thing was that I ended up holding totally different theological ideas – but I never had the privilege of long theological debates with him. I came to despise all things dispensational, for instance. And my reading of Scripture never led me to adopt his strong male leadership positions. It would have been fun to debate my hero on these and other issues. But, to this day, I've never lost my love or respect for Coach Lindgren.

I remember on one occasion deciding that I most definitely loved Jesus but I did not like Christians or the Christian church. I suddenly decided that I didn't like the Bible too much either. I made a commitment about a month or two after beginning college that I would personally debunk the Bible and the church (I know, I know… there are few things more arrogant than a college freshman who after two thousand years of the most brilliant minds in human history, I was going to debunk the whole thing in my spare time). I wouldn't deny the reality of Jesus Christ. I couldn't - because I knew him. I'd actually met him and personally (existentially) experienced the living Christ - so I couldn't deny him. But as far as the Christian church and the Bible goes, I had decided that they were manmade and messed up and not worth our time. Needless to say, I never succeeded in this mission. For one thing, "I never got around to it, ok?" I got busy with the ski season and simply didn't have any time or energy to make any progress in my "debunking Christianity" project. I think I figured that I would pick it up in the Spring when the snow melted. I never got around to it because of a girl I met that year.

During the fall and into the winter, I kept running into this fellow student at Rockmont, a short brunette named Karen Kay Kindschy – one of the few cute girls at this school, in my humble opinion. I thought it was funny because my girlfriend at the time, on the ski racing circuit, was also named Karen Kay. Looking back years later, I could say these two "Karens" represented two different directions in life, a sort of fork in the road. Well, regardless, one thing led to another and I started hanging out with the short Christian Karen from the small Christian college. We got to know each other and I learned that her dad was a pastor. During the late Winter of my freshman year, she invited me to attend her church every Sunday and also to join her and her family at home after church for Sunday dinner. As she had told me, her father, Gaylord Kindschy, was the pastor of that church and had been since its beginning in 1955. That meant that Karen had been there at that church since she was born in 1958. In fact, she had actually lived in the church basement for the first year and a half of her life (which was the church parsonage). She still works in the basement helping teach the little children the Bible every Sunday. I often joke with people who visit the church: "she's been in the basement for 60 years. We don't let her upstairs very often." Well, as I'm sure you've guessed by now, I began attending Amazing Grace Church forty years ago, married the pastor's daughter, became a pastor myself, and I'm still there.

First, however, we return to my college freshman project to debunk and discredit the church and the Bible. My project never got off the ground because after a few weeks attending this ordinary church something strange happened - almost imperceptibly: my faith began to grow. It was as if there was this little seed of faith deep within me that had been dormant for many years but now began to grow. When I first entered the church, Amazing Grace Church, I experienced an even more radical culture shock than I had when I entered Rockmont College. The atmosphere at Amazing Grace was old-fashioned, multi-cultural, multi-racial, multi-generational, and fairly "charismatic" (I had no clue what that meant). The church was full of older church ladies who would come up to me and welcome me enthusiastically by smothering me with church hugs. I couldn't understand the sermons or the songs or the prayers (everyone seemed to pray at the same time – which kind of freaked me out). But for some odd reason, my faith began to grow week by week. To this day I often say, "I was hugged back into the faith by large church women." Going to church every Sunday literally saved my life and restored my faith. Once again, my experience deeply shaped my theology. To this day, I consider church attendance a life and death matter. Hence, this book which you hold in your hands.

Within a year or so, I had become a regular part of the church family at Amazing Grace Church and had even begun to co-teach the junior high boys' Sunday School class. I soon began to help out around the church in every way imaginable and even began to sing in the church choir - which was hard to believe if you knew how bad I was at singing. Among my family, it was well known that my third-grade teacher, Mrs. Bridges, had me sit down and not participate whenever the class stood up to sing. I never sang again for the next fourteen years – not until the day the choir director at Amazing Grace

Church told me to come up and join the group (her name was Sister Barlow - we called everyone brother or sister in our church). I was put in the bass section next to Gaylan Kindschy, Jack White, Terry Stratman, and Dick Wiseman. Next to them, I could actually sing the bass part reasonably well. In addition to beginning my long and illustrious singing career (ha!), I soon began to fall in love with theology - a love affair that has continued unabated for forty years.

It also wasn't long before I had developed a strong sense that I was part of a family at Amazing Grace. If I ever did forget that all important truth, I would receive a passionate reminder from the pastor's daughter. I'll never forget the Wednesday evening I stayed in my college dorm room studying instead of going to the mid-week church service. Later that evening, the front door of our apartment flew open and Karen (all five feet tall and full of righteous indignation) walked in uninvited, stormed right past my roommates (Paul, Dave, and Esbardo), into the hall and into my bedroom where she found me sitting on the top bunk. She came over to the bunk bed, stood between my dangling feet, and pointed her little finger in my face, and said with the fury and passion of John the Baptist: *"When the doors of the church are open, YOU BE THERE!! Are you part of this family or not?"* I never forgot that prophetic attack. We often joke around the church: "Karen isn't always able to attend every church service or event, but Joe has never missed a single one since that infamous Wednesday night assault."

The funny thing is, I actually agreed with her basic point – and still do - (however harshly it was delivered) and that message actually developed and fermented into the message of this book.

As I said, I married that bossy college student, graduated from college (a Business degree from the University of Denver), graduated from Seminary (an "enriched" M.A. in Systematic Theology from Denver Seminary), and entered full-time pastoral ministry as a pastor of Amazing Grace Church. Along the way we had four children (three sons and then finally a girl). Over the years, I continued to develop a love for the Lord and his church. I continued to love theology, preaching, teaching, and the study of Scripture. We got busy with parenting, coaching, work, ministry, and all the rest of life. Before we had time to look around and catch our breath, thirty-five years had flown by and our four children were not only raised and college educated (many with graduate degrees), three of them were married and, at last count, we had eight grandchildren. All fifteen children, counting the spouses, come to church each Sunday. They love the Lord, love their church family, love their parents, and love each other. They all then come over to the house for Sunday dinner. It's crowded, hectic, loud, and chaotic. And it all makes me think that I might be the luckiest man in America. During the three hours of doing the dishes and putting the house back together in the aftermath of a tornado, all I can say is: *my cup runneth over*.

During those early years at Amazing Grace Church, I grew up in the Christian faith and began to serve others as a teacher, camp counselor, camp director, deacon, and in any other area as needed. I also began to sense a calling to gospel ministry. At first, my interests were more academic. I was so in love with theology and teaching that I had decided to go to Denver Seminary and then pursue a PhD in Theology - most likely in Europe. Eventually, I entered Seminary and continued to assume I'd continue on to post-graduate studies. I designed my Master's program with that in mind - earning an "enriched" M.A. - which meant that I took all the languages I could: Hebrew, Greek, and Theological German. I also took all of the preaching courses. During my years in seminary, however, three things happened that derailed my academic dreams. First, by the time I graduated I had two young sons. Second, my family had needs and I was running out of time, energy, and money to meet those needs. Thirdly, and most importantly, I was sensing an equally strong love (and, I think, a calling) for my local church and for the practical ministry of pastoral care and the prayer, study, preaching, teaching, and spiritual direction it required. So, I began to transition towards being a general practitioner rather than an academic specialist. I would never lose my first love of doing theology, though, and I remain a passionate "arm chair" theologian to this day.

Earlier, I mentioned that the pastor of Amazing Grace Church when I arrived was Gaylord Kindschy. He became my mentor in the pastoral vocation and later my co-pastor and colleague. Little did I know at first, I happen to have hit the pastor/mentor lottery when I stumbled into the church. Pastor Kindschy turned out to be a walking, talking, living, breathing embodiment of Eugene Peterson's pastoral model. So, along with digesting every word Peterson wrote, I had the exquisite blessing of a daily apprenticeship with a master craftsman. To this day, I believe that the best way to learn how to be a pastor is to come alongside a wise veteran of the craft and walk with them every day for many years. As it turned out, Pastor Kindschy was the wisest of the wise men of our day, a pastor of pastors, a master of the craft, a true Spirit-filled, Christlike shepherd of his flock. As I write these words, he is 88 years old, in his sixty-fifth year of faithful service to the same congregation, and still an active member of the elder board. Indeed, my cup runneth over from the very beginning.

"WELL, OF COURSE YOU DO"

I experienced a phenomenon during my seminary training that deeply shaped my ecclesiology and my philosophy of ministry. I would often ask my fellow students where they went to church. Over and over and over I would receive the same reply: "Cherry Hills." My fellow students would almost always say it with a "duh" kind of tone: "well, duh!? Cherry Hills, of course!" or "HELLO??? Where do you think?" I would invariably ask them, "why?" And, again, they would answer with the same tone: "duh! It's the best church in town. Shouldn't we learn from the best?" To which I would respond, "well, not necessarily. Odds are, you're going to end up in a regular, ordinary church out in some place like Bugtussel, Kansas, or in some ugly neighborhood here in town. So, wouldn't you want to learn how to do life and ministry with ordinary people in an ordinary church?" Then I would almost always add, "besides, an ordinary church would love to have a seminarian around. Can you imagine what a blessing just one committed gifted seminary student (and their family) would be to a regular church?" Finally, after a while, I gave up and my stock answer became a simple "Well, of course you do." They usually didn't catch my sarcasm. I use that phrase to this day. By the way, just so you know, Cherry Hills was, and is, a fine church and I very much respected its long-time pastor (who recently retired and has since passed away). This conviction of mine about the "glory of the ordinary church" is not a criticism of Cherry Hills or any other church.

Over the years, the "new hot church" in town would change names. For a while in Southwest Denver a few churches took over the top spots – at least until they began to lose their members and their youth to the latest hot church. I've talked to pastors of churches in our city that once were growing rapidly and are now in decline. One of them said to me, "I'm losing all my members to the latest hot church. For years, I was the one stealing members from all the surrounding churches. At the time, I preferred to use the word ‘reaching’ rather than ‘stealing’ but now that it’s happening to me, it doesn’t feel so good.” Recently, in the Denver area, a couple of new names have taken over the top spot on the podium of public perception and have become the place “where everybody goes.” Hardly a week goes by when I don’t run into someone who mentions that they go to the new popular church - to which I always reply, “well, of course you do.” I’ve yet to run into someone who actually catches on to my sarcasm (thankfully). They take me literally as though it makes perfect sense that they would go to that church. Nowadays churches are usually called something cool like Cross Point, High Point, Green Point, Center Point, or Grace Point. I’ve yet to find a “Low Point Church.” This is no criticism of any church with one of those names or any other name. I just get a kick out of how cool church names are these days - I have a collection but I will spare you. Well, ok, just a few more of my favorites: “Epic,” “Flow Church,” “The Experience,” “The Spot,” “MyChurch,” and “H20 Church.”

My sister experienced the same phenomenon when she moved to Sacramento years ago. She and her husband designed and built a stunningly beautiful home in a gated community in Granite Bay, California. They soon became part of a good church nearby but they learned almost right away that they must have chosen the “wrong” church. They ran into neighbor after neighbor who attended a different church than my sister's. She found out that if her neighbors attended a church, they attended the super popular church in the area. They would say it in that same tone of "well, duh… of course." The underlying assumption seemed to be: Where else would we go? Everybody goes there. Everybody knows it's the place to go - the socially and politically correct place to attend. When my sister would tell them she already had another church home, they would look down and quickly change the subject. I've received that same response almost weekly for forty years when people ask me where my I go to church (and where I am the pastor). After I say, "Federal and Hampden," I am met with stunned silence while the person is thinking of something nice to say. After a long, cold, dead stare, I usually receive something like shocked pity or embarrassed confusion before the person quickly changes the subject. It's like they just discovered that you married your cousin from Arkansas and that you have five broken cars sitting on your front lawn next to your broken TV. I finally taught my sister my secret response, "well, of course you do."

I'll never forget the day that President Obama came to Denver and spoke a block away from Amazing Grace Church. On the news that night they showed the President speaking and they said that he had visited the most "impoverished" section of the Denver metro area. It made me smile and I got a kick out of telling that story many times over the years. I would also add something like, "we go to church in the part of town where Jesus would hang out" and other things that made me feel better about myself. It also reminded me, however, why people make that funny face whenever I tell them where our church is located. So, beginning way back in my seminary days when a hundred fellow seminary students all went to the same church together, whenever I hear that hundreds of my Christian friends and neighbors are all going to the same church here in Denver, I have the same response I've always had. Feel free to borrow the phrase and use it any time you want: **"**Well, of course you do**."**

> Allow me to hop up on my soap box just for a moment or two. The sad thing, of course, about everyone going to the latest hottest church, is that there are wonderful ordinary churches all over town that get ignored or abandoned. They live faithfully and patiently in the shadow of the latest hot spot. They are full of the glory of God if one will stop and take a long and loving look at them. Just to give one example from the Denver metro area: there is a church in the southwest area called *Foothills Fellowship Church*. It's a fine church and its pastor, ***Ed Tafilowski***, is one of the finest pastors in the state of Colorado. He has no idea that I've been admiring him from a distance for decades. Yet, for the most part, Pastor Ed and his church fly under the radar, decade after decade. This is the very kind of pastor and church that seminaries should

be promoting to their students. Unfortunately, though, most seminaries ignore these ordinary churches with their extraordinary pastors. I also know this to be true because I've observed another excellent pastor (Pastor ***Gaylord Kindschy***) serving faithfully in another excellent church in the Denver area for sixty-five years. Pastor Kindschy is truly one of the finest pastors in the country and serves in a church located just five minutes away from a nearby seminary (a seminary that I love - my Alma Mater). Pastor Kindschy's church has even financially supported this nearby seminary, monthly, for over thirty years. Believe me, they have no idea that Pastor Kindschy (or Amazing Grace Church) even exists. But, don't think twice, it's alright.

AMAZING GRACE: AN ORDINARY CHURCH

Amazing Grace Church is a non-denominational Protestant church with roots in the evangelical and charismatic movements. It is mildly charismatic (some would say very mild, others have left because it's too wild) and mildly liturgical (again, some say very mild, others have left because it's too liturgical). It's also a missions-minded, theologically rich, community church. CAVEAT: I'm using all of those terms in their best sense. I am fully aware that many of these descriptive terms (especially evangelical and charismatic) carry with them a boatload of negative connotations (all well-deserved, I might add). I do not identify myself or our church with the negative and ugly aspects of the charismatic and evangelical sub-cultures. What I mean by *charismatic,* is "respectful of the Holy Spirit's power and presence in life and ministry." By *evangelical,* I mean "we seek to live and proclaim the beautiful good news of Jesus Christ." Amazing Grace Church is an ordinary church, a "regular" church of regular size. It is a multi-generational family church, mostly blue collar, middle class and lower middle class, with a few slightly richer folks and a few near the poverty level. Most of the people, however, are just regular folks living from paycheck to paycheck, if they're lucky. The church is in a fairly impoverished section of town on a busy highway – surrounded by government subsidized housing, pawn shops, liquor stores, used car lots, and recently several cannabis dispensaries. We've been fortunate to be able to serve our neighbors and to love on the families in the neighborhood for almost seven decades. We truly see our calling as *a family of God on a mission*.

Several years ago, my dad was in town and visited the church. Right after arriving, he remarked, "This place is actually *amazing*! There are so many different types of people here." That was a wonderful complement about our fellowship. We liked it that way back then and we like it that way today. Just this week I was told again by a visitor, "this church is wonderful in that it has older people in it, but not *just* older people. It has lots of young people too. People of all types and ages!" Our church does many things wrongly and many things poorly. But we do get a few things right. For the most part, we do live up to our name, "Amazing Grace." As we put it on our website:

> *Our mission is to be a safe haven of grace in a world filled with "ungrace," a place marked by Christlike acceptance. We want you to come as you are. We seek to give each other the room to grow, the freedom to think, the safety to ask questions, and the time and space to develop in your giftedness. We want to be an encouragement toward those with past failures or current issues, but who are seeking forgiveness, counsel, and help in their struggle. We want Amazing Grace to be more than a song that we sing. We want it to be our defining characteristic.*

Earlier in the book, I mentioned the societal benefits of the rich and poor worshipping together, sharing sacred meals together, experiencing genuine fellowship together, and going through life together. I saw this beautifully fulfilled in our church. On countless occasions I witnessed wealthy friends of mine come alongside the poorest and loneliest members in our church and befriend them in deep and beautiful ways. I watched friends (like Rod and Jack and Tim, just to name a few) help people who were all alone. They helped them move and fix up their place and supply it with furniture and supplies. I watched them take them to events and include them in holiday gatherings. This would have a tremendous effect on all involved.

Let me give one example of how this works. Over sixty years ago, a lady named Arlene White came to our church. She had been raised among native Americans on the plains of Kansas. She literally grew up in tents (and teepees). She was almost completely ignorant of societal norms here in the big city of Denver. Simple things like how to properly talk and dress in public (like when and how to wear a bra!), and how to fix one's hair, etc., were unknown to her. But she began to participate regularly in the life of the congregation. Before long, she was all cleaned up and became a much beloved leader in our church. She sang often in our services, she was prayer warrior, she took care of many of the babies and children growing up in the church, she was a devoted wife and mother, she helped in countless areas of the church, and was a blessing to the church and neighborhood for the next fifty years.

What have I learned from being in one regular ordinary church all of my life? Hands down, without a doubt, the lesson I cherish most is this: *There's glory in the ordinary*. God's amazing glory is found in the ordinary mundane everyday run-of-the-mill people and places. God's glory dwells in ordinary vessels. Always has. Always will. All it takes is for us to look at our ordinary church family with new eyes. All it takes is a long and loving look with eyes that have been transformed by

Jesus Christ and his Holy Spirit. Starting with Abraham, to Moses and the formation of Israel, from David's rag tag army to Jesus in a manger, from poor and marginalized Israel to poor and marginalized followers of Christ... God has always chosen the out of the way obscure ones. God has always done things this way. Why would he change now? Eugene Peterson has preached this truth and written about this truth so often and so powerfully, I can't even remember when and where I first heard it. It goes something like this:

The "I love Jesus but not the church" crowd has been around from the very beginning. Church leaders have had to defend the church from the start. One of the more illustrious defenses of the church is a quote often attributed to Augustine: "The church is a whore, but she's my mother." As far as I can tell, Augustine never said it quite like that but he did say something similar in one of his sermons on the church:

> *Let us honor her, because she is the bride of so great a Lord. And what am I to say? Great and unheard of is the bridegroom's gracious generosity; he found her a whore, he made her a virgin. She mustn't deny that she was once a whore, or she may forget the kindness and mercy of her liberator.*

One poet put it this way: *"I could believe in Christ if he did not drag behind him his leprous bride, the Church."* Over the centuries, there have been countless people who thought that Jesus married beneath himself. People have always found it easier to love Christ than to love his bride. As I said, it's been this way from the very beginning. Let us never forget the common reaction to Jesus:

Later Jesus and his disciples were at home having supper with a collection of disreputable guests. Unlikely as it seems, more than a few of them had become followers. The religion scholars and Pharisees saw him keeping this kind of company and lit into his disciples: "What kind of example is this, acting cozy with the riffraff?" Jesus, overhearing, shot back, "Who needs a doctor: the healthy or the sick? I'm here inviting the sin-sick, not the spiritually fit." (Mark 2:15-17 - MSG)

The community forming around Jesus reminds us of the group forming around David in ancient Israel:

All those who were in distress or in debt or discontented gathered around him,
and he became their commander. About four hundred men were with him. (I Sam. 22:2)

According to Eugene Peterson, if we use our imaginations and view this as kind of an embryonic form of the people of God, we see a community full of stressed out people, up to their eyes in debt (probably running from people they owed money to), unhappy and depressed. Sounds like an ordinary church to me. A congregation of misfits in need of a Savior. Many of them did grow up, however. After ten years of living together, eating together, praying together, and fighting together, David's motley crew had developed into "David's mighty men." They had tremendous camaraderie and were full of courage and loyalty. This has always been the way of salvation and this is how God's people have always looked: *not defined mostly by where they came from but by what God did in them and for them and through them.*

As the apostle Paul wrote to one of those early Christian congregations (in my own paraphrase):

> *"not many of you were considered hotshots in the world. You had very little influence in society. You weren't the celebrities or the ones with power. God chose the lowly things of the world to shame the high society things. He chose the despised things to shame the popular things. He chose those who had nothing to shame those who had it all. He chose the losers of society to shame the winners. He chose the nobodies to shame the somebodies."*
> I Cor. 1:26-28 JSB version

If God has *always* chosen to work this way, does it really make sense that he would suddenly change his strategy?? No, I think it would be wise to assume that he still works this way.

He's still in the business of creating miracles that don't look like miracles – miracles like the church – like this *Amazing Grace Church* – a miracle in the form of the powerless, the vulnerable, the unimportant – not so very different from any random congregation you'd find anywhere else in the world. And it's our job to look around at each other and marvel at the glory of the ordinary – at the miracle of *us* – at this creation of the Holy Spirit called church or congregation. And not just any church or congregation: this congregation: *Amazing Grace Church on South Federal Boulevard.*

I've often said to my two church secretaries over the years, "hey, we've sure had some interesting characters in this church!" They would both invariably respond, "yeah! Like us!" Yeah, like us. I had to admit. Too many of us characters to mention. The names roll off our tongues like our very own "hall of fame." Here's just a brief sample:

- ***Sister Jonas*** and her goats. Believe it or not, our church is across the street from a place called "goat hill."

- ***Randy Minter***: Cerebral Palsy and a wonderful zest for life and for the summer camp.

- ***Arlene White***: who had a dog named Duke that never missed a church service – through rain or snow - even came when church was canceled, and just sat by the door.

- ***Brother Haraldsen***: our very own World War II vet, Battle of the Bulge, local hero. (All of which he reminded us of each week – and we loved him for it.) Ironically, he was passionately anti-war.

- ***Ray Alvarado***: our other World War II vet, recipient of the Purple Heart, whose funeral casket was surrounded by a world class Mariachi band. Former singer at Casa Bonita.

- ***June Jones***: came in through the back door on a Wednesday night, smoked like steam engine, called every Christian celebrity in the nation and befriended them, and won our hearts with her loyal encouragement. She befriended Philip Yancey, for instance, and Philip attended her funeral at our church – resulting in Philip and I becoming ski buddies.

- ***Patty Stratman***: She brought flamboyance into the church. In church skits or announcements, she'd dress up like cupid or a wild-west saloon woman and make us all laugh to the point of tears.

- ***Debbie Hamon***: as faithful and loyal as the night is long and known for her unique singing style. Some have even suggested that we've lost some visitors over her singing – which is just fine with us. We wouldn't want them around anyway. **If she ain't welcome, ain't nobody welcome.**

- ***Shirley Peterson***: cowboy singer, bus driver, and a 5th degree blackbelt in OCD.

- ***Dave Hart***: part hippie, part John McArthur, part John the Baptist.

- ***Greg Preston***: stepped right out of an old Hollywood western right into our hearts and lives. My grandson lived next door to him and thought he was Mr. McGregor in Peter Rabbit.

- ***Tina***: She'd scream out the "S" word, now and then, right in the middle of the sermon – just to make sure everyone was awake. After service, she'd steal the worship leader's phone and hide in the women's bathroom. You can't make this stuff up.

- ***Our unforgettable neighbors***: Robert E. Lee, Ursula, and countless others.

Around thirty years ago, early on in my ministry, I realized that a big part of my life calling was going to be loving and serving a large group of widows and elderly ladies in our church. I'm not sure why this group formed into such a large and powerful network of single women fiercely devoted to one another and to our church. One theory is that Pastor Kindschy's temperament (cautious, private, fatherly), along with his deep and profound integrity, made these women feel safe and welcome in his presence. I, on the other hand, was like an adopted son to these dear women. This group of widows became my close friends, my surrogate mothers, my mentors, and my fellow Bible students. We would get together almost every week for visits, coffee, prayer, and Bible studies. One by one, I would have the high and holy privilege to walk with them through the valley of the shadow of death. One by one, I would say goodbye to my good friends: Lena Perkins, Harriet Waybrew, Grace Walstrom, Bessie Cooper, Nora Lyons, Odessa Howard, Margaret Kratzer, Peggy Alverson, Ida Butterworth, Laverne Duke, Janet Carey, Verna Fletcher, Creta Mellema, Maxine McComas, Carol Baltimore, Eileen Tietze, Blanche Davis, Gerry Warner, Florence VanSkiver, Pearl Koenig, Peggy Cutter, Opal Haraldsen, Esther Newell, Betty Keaton, Edna Stanfield, Arlene White, Rosetta Grant, Irma West, Eddie Johnson, Mary Campbell, Rowena Yarbrough, Shirley Peterson, LaVaughn Gillespie, and Ruby Grubb, just to name a few. Any day spent with these precious saints was a day well spent. If I do nothing more in my life than love on these dear older sisters (mostly widows) and be loved by them, it will have been a life well lived.

Some of these families have been with us from the very beginning. Ruth Shepherd, for instance, is still part of our church family. She's part of the original "Grandma Bryson" clan and she was here in March of 1955 when Pastor Kindschy arrived. There's our dear sister Carrie Campbell who married into the Bryson clan (marrying Stan). There's Dan and Renee and Marlita, part of the Ken Haraldsen clan. There's all the others that are still here after many decades: Joanne Hughes, Dan Miller, Karen Reed, Debbie Hamon, the Vigils, Lehls, Sundgrens, Wisemans, Gardners, Careys, Mary Garza, Barbie Cunningham, Barbara Novy and her mother, Bonnie Dietz, the Schwartzs, Woodwards, Thurstons, Lewises, Beaches, Kindschys, Oesterreichs, Jacobs, Jakels, Pattersons, Prestons, Blairs, Zimmermanns, Baltimores, Marcojos, Guenthers, Rosanne DiCamillo, Bailey Sterling, Cathy Lamb Gonzales, Merry Davis, John McCoy, Emily Alvarado, Bryan Federowicz, Justin Pulford and the "newer" families: Hybinette, Kalkus, Rugley, Sawyer, Blankenship, Alirez, Coyle, Crystal, Quinn, Phelps, Lesh, Labreche, Sutton, Theander, Wilson, Ebel, Hernandez, Kissinger, Mallon, Priest, and Henning. These families are beginning to collect their own stories and beginning to add them to the church's legacy.

Serving this ordinary church, Amazing Grace Church on South Federal Boulevard, turned out to be my life calling. Going *together through life* with these people turned out to be my high and holy calling. **This place. These people. These families.** That's why every word Eugene Peterson ever wrote was written to me. That's why every one of his words seem to ring true in my heart and experience, almost like they were written in my soul. They were like burning coals pouring off the page. Sorry, I lost control there for a moment and just started talking like Dylan. I couldn't help it. Anyway, what I meant was that Eugene Peterson speaks my heart – precisely - when he writes: **"I realized that this was my place and work in the church."**

CHAPTER FIVE

Health Club, Half-way House, Hospital, or Home?

"The quickest way to get home is to stay there."

- Zack Eswine

In Philip Yancey's insightful book, *Church, Why Bother?* he attempts to give an answer to his own question (don't all of his marvelous books do the same thing?). He describes his childhood experiences growing up in a graceless, fundamentalist church. He ended up leaving the church for a period of time during which he didn't see many reasons to bother with church. Finally, though, he found himself returning to a local church and to regular participation in its common life and worship. At first, he experienced fairly severe culture shock just like I had when I returned. He found himself surrounded by a diverse family of believers made up of people quite unlike himself - and people quite different than those he would naturally hang around. The music, the dress, the vocabulary - it was a different world than the academic, high-society, classical music world he had grown accustomed to. It was this shocking, visible difference of worlds, however, that soon became one of Yancey's most appreciated qualities of an ordinary church. To witness how a common faith in Christ could draw together, and hold together, a diverse group of people that had little else in common, was a powerful experience. He slowly realized that the church did not exist primarily *for* him - that God was the audience (and not us) - that the church gathered first to worship God. Yancey writes, "we should leave a worship service asking ourselves not 'what did I get out of it?' but rather 'Was God pleased with what happened?'" He went on to write, "Church exists primarily not to provide entertainment or to encourage vulnerability or to build self-esteem or to facilitate friendships but to worship God; if it fails in that, it fails."

Before giving several good reasons why we might "bother" with church, Yancey first emphasized the need for a grace-filled community. He'd had his fill, for one lifetime, of judgmentalism, legalism, and hatred. He purposefully looked for a church full of people unlike himself that exhibited the marks of a grace-filled family. He returned to church. He had reached the settled conclusion that one can only follow Christ as part of an actual congregation of believers, a family of fellow pilgrims. He quotes Paul Tournier, "There are two things we cannot do alone, one is to be married and the other is to be a

Christian." Yancey came home by coming back to a family.

You can probably tell by now that *family* is my favorite metaphor for the local church. There are, of course, many other metaphors we could use. In Scripture, the church is referred to as a body, a bride, a branch, a city, a tree, a vineyard, a field, a building, a temple, an army, and others. Paul uses at least four of these in one letter to the Corinthians. Brian Zahnd, in his book, *Beauty Will Save the World*, suggests another in his chapter entitled, "A Shelter From the Storm" (which he got from Isaiah 4, Isaiah 25, Isaiah 32, the Sermon on the Mount, and, of course, Bob Dylan). In that chapter, he points out that certain metaphors can be more helpful at certain times (and less so at other times). For instance, we may want to minimize our use of the "army" metaphor in our current cultural milieu - both here and around the world. All of these metaphors, remember, can and should be applied to the local church - and not just to the church in general. As I pointed out in Chapter Three, each local church is not just a *part* of the body of Christ. Each *is* the body of Christ, each is *the* family of God, each church can and should be *the shelter from the storm* in its neighborhood. Zahnd connects the beginning and end of Jesus' Sermon on the Mount - the beatitudes and the house built on solid rock - and teaches that when the church is a shelter amidst a world of violence, revenge, and un-grace, it welcomes the poor in spirit, comforts those who mourn, esteems the meek, hungers for justice, extends mercy, is pure in heart, majors on peacemaking, and endures persecution. I agree wholeheartedly. But, in the end, my favorite metaphor remains: the church as *family*.

There is a problem, however, with my favorite metaphor. Many people remind me that it's not always easy to feel at home within a church family. Many people find it difficult to make long and lasting connections with people in a local church. Others discover, unfortunately, that the church is indeed very much like their own family: the place where they get hurt and ignored and betrayed and abused. Sadly, they find that they can experience as much (or more) relational pain and suffering within the church than outside of it. Sarah Bessey puts it this way: "Some of my greatest wounds have come from church, and so, my greatest healing has happened here too."

What then of my favorite metaphor? I have no quick and easy answer (although I devote the next chapter to giving it my best shot). I have only hope that maybe, over time, an ordinary church (and maybe *only* an ordinary church) can provide people a place to belong and a place to come home to. Maybe an ordinary church can best provide the context for developing and expressing patience, forgiveness, grace, and reconciliation.

CHURCH AS HEALTH CLUB

There was a man in Denver named Gene Cisneros who ran a

health club several years ago (and maybe still does). He was interviewed in the Denver Post. I was very impressed by his business philosophy because it mirrored what I feel is a biblical philosophy of ministry.

One of the main frustrations in pastoral ministry is the constant pressure – both from the world *and* the church – to base local church ministry on programs, products, and performances. In other words, we as pastors are judged to be successes or failures based on our ability to build and lead an organization that offers excellent programs, products, and performances to an ever-increasing customer base (or market share). People don't use those words, of course. We, instead, refer to the customers as "seekers" whom we are "reaching" for the Lord. The "customers," likewise, use better sounding language. They might say things about the church such as, "my kids love it there!" or "I really love their music," or, negatively, "I'm just not being fed by the teaching ministry," or "our church just doesn't have much of a youth group right now," or "I like that they offer a Saturday night service so we can use Sunday for family stuff." Let's return to that health club in Denver.

Gene Cisneros began his little health club over thirty years ago. He named it Kinetic Fitness Studio. His club is located in the north Cherry Creek area of Denver and is described by the interviewer as a "quite simple, small, and even shabby little gym hidden down a back alley." Nearby are several popular top-of-the-line gyms with all the bells and whistles, packed with customers. Gene and his little gym, however, have somehow managed to help all kinds of folks get in shape while, at the same time, training Denver's boldest, biggest names in the civic and financial worlds. So, Gene was asked, "what's your secret?" His answer was fascinating:

> *I just wanted to open a place to work out. I didn't want all that foo-foo stuff. It's pretty primitive in terms of the facility. It's only 3,000 square feet; we have some TV's. I didn't even have a drinking fountain for eight years. To this day, there are no showers. No lockers. No steam. No sauna. This is bare bones. But if people want to get in shape and they're serious about it, they come to my club. We do have state-of-the-art equipment. But we have no membership director; we don't have a contract. I had every reason to fail. But people just come in and we go, "let's get to work."*

I would sum up Gene's philosophy this way: they major on the essentials: knowing what they're about - getting in shape - and establishing genuine relationships. Gene said, "*Oh, yes. I can't tell you how many members have gotten married. Dozens. In a club this size, everybody knows everybody.*"

Every summer for thirty years, I've provided tennis lessons for children in my neighborhood. For better or worse, my philosophy is similar to Gene's. After coming across this interview, my reaction was, "Hey! His approach is the same as my approach with the tennis lessons! I have no bells, no whistles, no gadgets, no contracts, no fancy marketing tools. I have no assistants. I really don't have a single fancy thing to offer these kids. But I have tons of kids who are dying to come back every summer and who bring all their friends. Why? Because I know what I'm doing and I know what we are about - the kids will learn to love and play tennis and they will become good friends with me and each other. I just plain love teaching kids." I thought, "this directly relates to our church and to our philosophy of ministry! This is exactly how we do church."

My wife is a member of a large, professional, polished, popular health club with all the bells and whistles. I said to her, "the problem with a club that's based on programs, products, and performances, is that it doesn't necessarily care about you as a person. In fact, by its very nature, it cannot. In a program/product/performance-based organization, people are simply numbers - "units" to be used to further the organization." I said to her, "If you leave and someone takes your place, the organization will continue to function just as well and its leaders will be just as happy. If you never actually use the club or get in shape, neither the organization nor its administrators really care. As long as you sign a contract and pay your money, they're satisfied."

I then went on to make the comparison with churches. If you base a church on offering programs, products, and performances to "religious customers," then your highest value and commitment must be in attracting enough people to the programs at any given point. As long as there are enough people and money coming through the system – at any given point in time (hopefully, an ever-increasing amount of people and money – "growth" is the Christian word we use for that) – then the officers of the organization are happy. Whether it's the same people or different ones, it doesn't necessarily have to matter to the board of directors (or, if you prefer: elders, deacons, trustees, presbytery, session, or whatever you call the board with ultimate power). Whether the individual people are growing or not, building life-long relationships or not, doesn't necessarily have to matter to the church's leaders. As long as more people and money are coming through the front door than people exiting the back door, the organization can survive (and maybe even thrive) in the eyes of the world and the church.

So, my five-part question: What if, on the other hand, our local churches were committed to

1. helping people grow "healthy in God, robust in love;"

2. helping people build life-long, multi-generational relationships in a committed community that is going

through life together;

3. creating a sacred space to meet together for prayer, the word of God, the Lord's Supper, Baptism, singing, fellowship, and common meals;

4. holding to a model of "pastor" as someone who knows the flock, cares for the flock, and loves the flock; and to…

5. being a "family on a mission" that is committed to loving God and Neighbor; and to making disciples – one at a time if necessary?

Halfway House Lessons on Love and Hate

Nearby our church, there's a halfway house for men who are nearing the end of their incarceration. One of the core families in our church lives in between the church and the halfway house. The father in that family is an interesting character. He looks like some cowhand from an old cowboy movie: a rough, tough, sixty-three-year-old man, dirt all over and skinny as a nail. He wears an old hat with a hole in it, smiles with crooked teeth, has one eye that works, two ears that don't, and loves to talk to anyone who walks by the place. Underneath that rough exterior is a very intelligent, thoughtful follower of Christ who loves to get in people's faces, (lovingly, of course) and ask them questions about their life. Around the church, we call it the "Gregg interrogation." We like to say, "If you get past the Gregg interrogation (and Debbie's singing), we know that you'll fit right in around here." By the way, Debbie gave me permission to say that. Neither she nor I are known for our singing ability at the church. Gregg just told me to slightly misspell his name so nobody would guess who I was talking about.

Well, one evening several years ago, one of the men from the halfway house was returning after work. The men from this halfway house are allowed to go to work and, sometimes, attend church, with very strict guidelines and rules. The man from our church met him on the street and began his loving interrogation. After spending some time to get to know the man and his story, Gregg asked him if he'd met Jesus while in prison. The man responded, "no, not really. I'd already met Jesus in Sunday School as a kid."

Our friend then asked him if he'd attended any churches yet since he'd arrived at the halfway house. The man said, "yes, just one. I attended a church not too far from here but it was bad. All the pastor did was rant and rave about how bad President Obama was and how he was ruining the country. He talked a lot about terrorism, too." The man then said something that I'll never forget. He said, "I don't need no preacher to tell me who to hate."

Those words reverberated around in my head. I can't seem to get away from them. *I don't need no preacher to tell me who to hate.* I knew he was right on. He most certainly did *not* need the help of any preacher in hating other people. None of us do. Nobody needs help hating people. It's natural and instinctive. Hating people – especially, hating our enemies - is as natural to us as breathing. It's what we do. It's what the world does. It's what our culture teaches us to do. It's the American way. It's the human way.

Here's the problem: it preaches well. It preaches really well! Some TV and radio talk show hosts have picked up on this and have turned it into a multi-billion-dollar industry. Many preachers have likewise picked up on this and learned that if you want to make people feel good about themselves and like you as a preacher… all you have to is identify some common enemies and let 'er rip. People will eat it up. And it has a double benefit. It thrills and satisfies the listener's hunger for hate while simultaneously providing an outlet for the preacher's own anger, insecurity, and fear. And if you think this is only a right-wing problem, think again. Hatred is flowing in both directions these days. Hatred and hypocrisy run both red and blue. Christians on both sides of the partisan political divide are quick to jump to conclusions and to join the latest verbal mob. For years, the right wing seemed to lead the way in this area but, lately, the left wing seems to be returning the favor (with gusto).

The problem is this: it might be the natural way, the human way, and the American way, but it's not the Jesus way. It's not the gospel way. It's certainly not the narrow way. And when we allow ourselves to take the easy way out, we are abandoning our posts and our calling. And we do it to our shame. As Eugene Peterson pointed out nearly thirty years ago, we pastors have taken vows of ordination that commit us to standards of integrity and performance that cannot be altered to suit people's tastes or what they are willing to pay for – especially people's tastes for hate and revenge. It's possible to view our angry preaching as "courageous" when it might well just be cowardly accommodation to a hate-loving constituency within our church and society.

What is the Jesus way? What is the difficult, narrow, gospel way to which we have been called? To paraphrase pastor Brian Zahnd in his book on radical forgiveness, "If Christianity isn't about forgiveness and enemy-love, it's about nothing at all**."** That's what I need a preacher to tell me. I need a preacher to tell me *who* to love and *how* to love. I need a preacher to tell me how to love my enemies, how to forgive those who have sinned against me, how to understand the "other"- the foreigner, the alien, the least, the last, the lost, and the little – and to exhort me to do unto them as I would have them do unto me.

I don't need no preacher to tell me who to hate.

This truth is just as true *within* the Christian camp. There is not only a natural hater in all of us, there is a natural (often hidden) fundamentalist in all of us. By that, I mean that we all have a strong desire to be in the right camp listening to the right preacher who interprets the Bible in the right way, reading the right books and attending the right conferences so that we will all end up using the right translation and believing the right things and saying the right things in the right way. Sadly, we're usually so *right* we're *wrong.*

There is a well-known radio teacher who specializes in this approach. Every now and then I will come across him preaching on the radio and I will invariably tell myself (in a very smug way), "time him: within five minutes he will be patting himself on the back for being one of the few preachers who preach 'the truth.' He will express his sadness about those who live in towns or neighborhoods that have no preachers courageous enough (like him) or faithful enough (like him) to preach the Bible correctly (translation: in a way that agrees with him)." I then, of course, reprimand myself for being so judgmental of judgmental preachers. Before long, however, I backslide again and come across the popular television preacher who does the same thing. This particular preacher has gained a huge following and built a huge empire by "courageously" and "boldly" preaching the "truth" (unlike all of those "wimpy-wishy-washy liberal preachers" out there). Most of his listeners, however, remain ignorant of the fact that he is actually spewing his own opinions (very weak opinions, I might add) while all the while giving the impression that he's thoroughly "biblical." After reprimanding myself once again for being so judgmental, I pray for the preacher and vow to be more careful (translation: watch only sports on TV).

We live in a world of un-grace. A world of revenge. A world of Dog-eat-dog competition. Violence, power, and pride. Celebrity worship. The church can serve as a half-way house between that kingdom of un-grace and the kingdom of grace, that is, the kingdom of Christ - a kingdom of citizens who love their enemies and value forgiveness, peace, and humility. The last thing a person needs when they encounter Christ's kingdom is a church that provides them with a new list of people to hate. The last thing they need is to have their worldly values endorsed and confirmed. If all they do when they enter the church is to enter a *Christianized* version of a world that hates its enemies and values competition, power, pride, success, money, celebrity worship, etc., they have gained nothing. They simply remain in a Christianized version of the world - the world *lite*, the world *decaffeinated*, the world *with a fish slapped on it*. When we follow the way of un-forgiveness and un-grace, it is most certainly *not* the way of Jesus. As Anne Lamott put it, "We know that we have made God into our own image when we discover that he hates all the same people we do."

I don't need no preacher to tell me who to hate.

CHURCH AS HOSPITAL

So, where are we? What is the church? So far, we've discovered that the church is a place to get healthy (or healthier) - a place to grow up as a human being. In that sense, it is a health club. Hopefully, it is a health club that actually cares about you and your growth: a fellowship of people that are committed to each other and to each other's fitness. A fancier way to put it: the church is the place where saints are made. And, yes, I do mean that. In the next chapter on the Church as a *family at worship* I will emphasize that the church is a school for character formation. But, for now, I want to make it clear: the church is also (and always) a half-way house for people who are just emerging from a life in prison, a life of bondage to sin and self, a life marred and scarred by all kinds of addictions. Maybe more important than anything, the church is for people making the transition from a world of revenge, competition, and ungrace to a new world of love, acceptance, and radical forgiveness. As the New Testament apostles put it, we are being saved from ourselves and from our old way of living. We are being transformed to a whole new way of living and thinking. The Apostle Peter says, “you were redeemed from the empty way of life...” (I Peter 1:18). Paul refers to us leaving behind our “former way of life” and “putting off our old selves” so that we can now “take hold of the life that is truly life” and enter a “new way of being human” (Eph. 2:10; 4:20, 22; I Timothy 4:19). All of this happens, of course, “now, through the church” (Eph. 3:10) - God’s divine half-way house full of recovering sin-addicts.

In that sense, the church is a hospital for broken and hurting people. I love Pope Francis’ description of the church as a “field hospital.” All of us, to some degree, are together on the dangerous battlefield of life, carrying weaknesses and sustaining wounds from all sorts of enemies, making mistakes in judgment, and at times succumbing to fear and cowardice. At any given point, we are all suffering together. At some point in our lives, we all need a field hospital to bandage us up and keep us alive. It is more than a cliché to say that the church is more of a hospital for sinners than it is a museum for saints. Even though our primary identity in Christ is that of *saints* (God’s dearly beloved holy ones), and even though we are absolutely committed to becoming more “saintly” (i.e. more like Christ), and even though “producing saints” is a primary calling of the church, we nevertheless remain fellow sinners, fellow pilgrims in this fallen and broken world. We never advance beyond our humble recognition of our common weakness. Like the members of a 12-Step recovery group, we are united, first and foremost, not by our strengths but by our shared weakness and by our utter dependence on Christ and each other. We never grow beyond a humble mutual confession of our sinfulness and of our common need for God's mercy and grace.

In Heather Kopp's delightful memoir, *Sober Mercies: How Love Caught Up With a Christian Drunk,* in the days following her time in rehab, she began to consider attending one of "those" recovery groups. She began to explore various meetings around her home town. On the north side of town, she discovered a group with a "more professional crowd:"

> *The room smelled of hand lotion and chewing gum. Some of the men wore ties, and I noticed several women with manicures. You could almost imagine that you were at a business meeting instead of a gathering of drunks.*

Heather then discovered other meetings that were closer to her home which was in the older section of town and closer to downtown. It reminded her that their differences - whether age, gender, race, socio-economic status - weren't as significant as their similarities. She found hope and healing by focusing on their shared weakness rather than their different strengths. The church, at its best, should function in much the same way. Philip Yancey has beautifully articulated this insight on numerous occasions. Brennan Manning and Richard Rohr have done the same. All three of these writers have come away from visiting a 12-Step group saying, “I just witnessed a holy place full of brutal honesty, sincere humility, radical forgiveness, total acceptance, and mutual accountability – all what church is supposed to be.” They were on holy ground and they knew it instantly. Oh, that our churches would manifest this kind of holiness (humility and honesty). Can you imagine what would happen if we all began every worship service with each person standing up and introducing themselves as, “Hi. My name is Joe and I’m a sinner. Apart from God’s power and apart from this fellowship, I’m lost. I’m powerless over sin.” I said this once in a sermon and my son, Andrew, reminded me, “Dad, we do that every Sunday. That’s why, in a good and true liturgy, we always begin with the prayer of confession. We confess our sins together at the beginning of every service.” I said, “ok, fine, there’s that I guess.”

Most of us discover, sooner or later, that we are all broken. Everything is broken. We also learn, however, that our common brokenness doesn’t need to lead to despair. We need constant reminders that it is our brokenness that not only brings us closer together, it is what brings us closer to God. It would be fair to say that a “saint” is a sinner who has let God and others in through the cracks, through the wounds. “Blessed are the poor in spirit, for theirs is the Kingdom of God.” God comes through the wounds. Or, as Leonard Cohen puts it, “there is a crack in everything, that’s how the light gets in.” Eugene

O'Neil put it this way:

Man is born broken. He lives by mending.
The grace of God is glue.

What I'm saying is that the church, at its best, is a family of broken people that desperately need each other. That's why I've always been a big fan of church members calling and writing whenever someone misses church for a couple of weeks. This is exactly what is happening when men and women in a recovery group worry about each other. We are supposed to worry about each other and check on each other. This Christian life, true Christian worship, is not designed to be a large spectator event into which we can anonymously drop in and out when and if we're in the mood or have the time – or a large shopping mall where we can shop when it suits us. We are supposed to care for one another and we are supposed to be concerned that nobody falls away, relapses, goes back out into a world of hatred and revenge, and drifts away from the body of Christ. As we read in Hebrews, "Let us consider how we may spur one another on towards love and good deeds, not giving up meeting together, as some are in the habit of doing" (Heb. 10:24-25). I think you know by now that in my humble (but accurate) opinion, tens of millions of American Christians suffer from this very bad habit.

THE CHURCH AS HOME

Finally, though, I return to my favorite metaphor. The church is to be our home - our family. This is so central to my experience and to my theological understanding that I've devoted the entire next chapter to the church as family. I believe that the church is our "first family" - taking precedence over all other relationships and commitments. Because of our common bond in Christ, and our shared commitment to him, our local church deserves our highest allegiance - beyond that of our allegiances to our country, our biological families, our jobs, our hobbies, and everything else. Please note: I am not advocating for some kind of sick sociological cult wherein some leader (or leaders) control every aspect of our lives. I am not suggesting that we drink anybody's "Kool-Aid" or blindly follow something or someone that contradicts the basic story of Jesus or violates our consciences or common sense. What I am saying is that our church home, our church family, should be just that. Nothing less, nothing more. A place to come home to. A family with whom to travel *together through life.*

THE THANKSGIVING TABLE

I've often thought that one way to communicate what I'm trying to say in this book is to compare the local congregation to our annual Thanksgiving dinner.

There's a recent article in Christianity Today about the Multi-site Church phenomenon going on in North America. Every time I hear about a multi-site church, I must admit that I get a queasy feeling in my gut. Something about the whole thing just doesn't make sense to me. I try to imagine that same phenomenon applied to our thanksgiving tables. When I hear about multi-site churches, this is the (sarcastic) parable that inevitably pops into my head:

> Imagine a person comes to your door one year with a proposal to make your family's Thanksgiving dinner a "franchise" of their more professional "Thanksgiving Table" organization. Imagine that the visitor explains that their organization has been very successful at putting on Thanksgiving dinners and, in fact, usually serves more than ten thousand people at their annual dinner at the main campus. They are very, very good at cutting the turkey and they have a person who gives a fantastic Turkey prayer and Thanksgiving speech. They pipe in great music and can help set the table for you. They can even bring in a person to help train you and your family in the weeks leading up to your big dinner. On Thanksgiving Day, they will send a staff member to your house to actually cook and cut your turkey. This staff member is a professional and will skillfully cut your turkey at tableside for all to watch. Then, when the time

comes for the head of the table to make a speech and give a prayer, we will actually bring to you our master speaker by satellite. You will be able to listen to the same world class Turkey speech and prayer that we get to experience at the main campus – all on a huge HD TV right at your table. Never again will you have to experience your own father or mother or grandparents with their mediocre attempts at making Thanksgiving Day speeches or their feeble attempts at Thanksgiving prayers. From now on, you will have only the best at your table. We can even go over your typical menu and eliminate the poorer dishes. In some cases, we have even been able to prevent some of your more undesirable relatives from attending. In our training, we will show you how to make your table much more attractive to visitors. If you follow our lead, you will have one of the better Thanksgiving dinners in your neighborhood and might even begin attracting many more people to attend your annual celebration. We've discovered that the average age of those attending your thanksgiving dinners will drop as you attract more and more people in their twenties and thirties.

We are not for a moment advocating that you "steal" people from the families that live nearby. We prefer the word "reaching." We like to say that you are "reaching" people who may not have a home for the holidays or who have grown bored or dissatisfied with their own family

> celebrations. We try not to be the judge of these people. We just don't think that these unfortunate souls should be forced to remain in their own boring families which may have become unbearably old-fashioned and outdated. It's unfortunate that these people leave their own family dinners but is not our fault. We like to look at it this way: in the *thanksgiving kingdom*, everyone wins as along as they're going somewhere and celebrating thanksgiving with someone. Hey, after all, you might be able to *reach* people that aren't even attending their own family's thanksgiving dinners. And, at the same time, there may still be a few old stick-in-the-muds that actually prefer to go to those old-fashioned, small, mediocre Thanksgiving dinners. They may still reach people that won't come to your hipper cooler dinner.

I hope the point of my sarcastic parable is obvious. I fully realize that there are thousands of wonderful committed Christians and leaders who are part of a multi-site church. I am certainly not condemning all aspects of this model nor am I judging all of its leaders. I also grant that there are exceptions and there may be situations where this is wise and effective. What I am saying is that a local congregation doesn't just need to hear a good preacher and good music. It needs to hear its *own* preachers – its own shepherds who know them and love them and who have shared life together with them. I love how Pastor Kwon from Washington, D.C., put it:

> *I'm thrilled whenever Christians are hungry for God's Word, but sermon podcasts should be a "snack" or "side," not the "main dish." We should receive God's Word primarily from preachers who know and love us; an over-reliance on celebrity preachers often breeds discontentment with local pulpits. Further, the hearing of God's Word should be an embodied discipline practiced primarily in the corporate gathering of the saints, not the privacy of one's earbuds. During "live" preaching, the Holy Spirit often moves in our midst in a unique, "you had to be there" way. We should want to be there! Podcasts [and satellite feeds] couldn't have produced the fruit of Pentecost.*

It's not just information alone that matters. There's more to being a Christian than just learning content. There's nothing wrong with engaging good content through books, blogs, and podcasts as a form of learning. But, as Skye Jethani puts it, "We should all still find ourselves accountable to a local congregation with local *incarnate* relationship-based authority." The men, women, and children in a local congregation need to share the word with each other, sing to one another, pray for one another, love one another... and so forth. Besides, one flaw of the multi-site model is that if taken to its logical conclusion, every congregation in the nation should be beaming in the same sermon from the same pulpit.

Likewise, we should have the same worship leader and worship team as well. If the goal is to share the same great preacher with several congregations at once, why not share the absolute best preacher in the country (and best worship team in the nation) with all congregations at once? It would be as if every church in the nation was a franchise of the same great church and everyone could have the same great experience. And, if we're going to go that far, why not just have everyone stay home and watch it on their own TV from their bed? Wait! Now that I think about it, millions of Christians have already figured that one out.

CHAPTER SIX

When the Church was a Family

"When the church was a family, the church was on fire."

- Joseph Hellerman

We are now at the center of my heart's passion about the local church. This chapter contains much of what I have been trying to say for over thirty years. I usually cannot contain this passion for long and it comes out in one form or another in most of my conversations, sermons, and lessons, along with any other time I get the chance. As I said at the outset, even a two-year-old girl picked up on my thoughts and feelings. I am fully aware that this passionate conviction is partly a result of my experience (it's all I've ever known) and also partly due to my temperament (I was born this way). But I also think (I hope) this passion comes from somewhere deeper than just my own experience. I believe the church was always meant to be a family. I believe God always intended to build his church and that his church would manifest itself in local families of believers who were radically committed to one another and to going *together through life*.

Hear me well: from the very beginning, the church was a family. It was well known from the first day of the church that nobody had to be alone. It was well known that baptism meant that a Christian's first identity, strongest allegiance, and highest loyalty was now attached to his or her local church family. It was one of the remarkable traits of the early church: everyone could have a family. Married or single, married or widowed, old or young, slave or free, male or female, Jew or Gentile, rich or poor, every person could be part of a family. It is to be the same today and it often is. In our own church, I've seen many people find a close family among us. Some of them would be completely alone in the world without their church family.

In my almost forty years of life and ministry at Amazing Grace Church I have been known for one main passion: *the church is a family* - and all that that entails. Because this message runs counter to our hyper-individualist, consumerist culture, I often felt like I was beating my head against a brick wall.

Joseph Hellerman is a New Testament scholar who has spent years studying the social structures surrounding Christians of the first century and the reality of the church as family in the New Testament. He found that the most important group for persons in the ancient world was the family and that it was no accident that the New Testament writers chose the concept of the family as the central social metaphor of the church. They intended Christians to be committed to each other in a congregation with the strongest interpersonal bonds imaginable. Hellerman's discoveries are profound and, I think, speak with prophetic urgency to our situation:

> *The New Testament picture of the church as a family flies in the face of our individualistic cultural orientation. God's intention is not to become the feel-good Father of a myriad of isolated individuals who appropriate the Christian faith as yet another avenue toward personal enlightenment. Nor is the biblical Jesus to be conceived of as some sort of spiritual mentor whom we can happily take from church to church, or from marriage to marriage, fully assured that our personal Savior will somehow bless and redeem our destructive relational choices every step of the way.... You may be surprised to discover that the expression "personal Savior" occurs nowhere in the pages of Scripture.... our radical overemphasis on a personal relationship with God is an American - not a biblical - theological construction.*

Is Hellerman (or I) denying that we have a personal relationship with God? Of course, not. The Christian faith is always personal. But it's never individualistic. And it's never *merely* personal. For many years, I have tried to communicate that the New Testament's "one another" commands only make sense in the context of a committed family. How can we truly love, accept, and forgive one another unless we have walked *together through life* long enough and committed enough (to have hurt each other enough) for those commands to make sense? I've often repeated the slogan, *the good times make us friends, the bad times make us family*. I personally believe that we grow best by working out our differences, working out our offenses, working on understanding one another, trying our hardest to accept one another, and so on. I believe that countless believers have left their church families too soon and too easily and have suffered the consequences of immaturity, bitterness, unforgiveness, and relational brokenness. After studying the family concept in the New Testament, Hellerman affirms that

> *Spiritual formation occurs in the context of community... long-term interpersonal relationships are the crucible of genuine progress in the Christian life.*

My suspicion is that one of the main reasons people are uncomfortable with an emphasis on the "church as family" is that it makes them feel "accountable" (in the short term) and "stuck" (over the long term). Many people have admitted to me over the years that they are very attracted to the anonymity of a megachurch. They tell me that when I teach on this subject it makes them feel like they must stay in the same church their entire life. They get the impression from me that they would be wrong to ever leave the church. Well, I must admit that I do believe it would be ideal, all things being equal, to go through life together as a family. But, no, I've never wanted people to view the church as a kind of "Hotel California" that they are stuck in for life against their will. I do believe that we should pursue the ideal (of together through life) whenever possible. There are many exceptions, of course, but I admit: I do believe it is almost always better to stay than to go. As I sometimes say, *there are a few good reasons to leave one's church family and a hundred bad ones*.

Over the years, I never cease to be amazed (and heartbroken) over how many close friends have suddenly just walked out my life and out of our church family's life - with no warning, with no conversation, and for no apparent reason. And I am not alone. Countless pastors have confirmed that they have experienced the same exact thing over and over and over. They too have been utterly baffled and heartbroken over these bizarre departures. They also confirm that usually, for some odd reason, it was usually their closest friends who mysteriously disappeared. They reported that for some reason, the people that abandoned them without even saying goodbye were almost always the ones who had received the bulk of their love, time, energy, and care over the years. And it's not just painful for those who are left behind feeling rejected and abandoned for no apparent reason; it is also (almost always) bad for the person who leaves the family in this manner. After spending over 60 years in the local church, I have come to believe in this maxim that emerged from Hellerman's study:

PEOPLE WHO STAY ALSO GROW.
PEOPLE WHO LEAVE DO NOT GROW.

Hellerman puts it this way: "It is a simple but profound biblical reality that we both grow and thrive together or we do not grow much at all." The radical individualism that is so rampant in our culture, including within the church sub-culture, leads to a life of *serial leaving*. Every time things get rough in the church or in the home, rather than stay and grow up, we tend to leave, withdraw, and try out something new. As Zack Eswine puts it, "The quickest way to get home is to stay there."

Allow me to repeat Alissa Wilkinson words:

> *Our Christian subculture is marked by church hopping. We stay put as long as it suits us, until we are offended, or decide we're not being "fed." So, wanting to quietly validate our own identities, we tend to silo ourselves into churches where everyone looks like us, talks like us, likes the same movies, and won't embarrass us in public. But what if we took a cue from popular culture's push for diversity and realized that surrounding ourselves with our duplicates only makes us more self-centered.*

Unfortunately, the family aspect of church is constantly at odds with the popular culture. It is a sad fact that one of the core values of American culture - *radical individualism* - turns out to be the great enemy of *church as family*. Again, Hellerman:

> We have been socialized to believe that our own dreams, goals, and personal fulfillment take precedence over the well-being of any group - our church or our family, for example - to which we belong. The immediate needs of the individual are more important than the long-term health of the group. *So, we leave and withdraw, rather than stay and grow up, when the going gets rough in the church or in the home...* The tune of radical individualism has been playing in our ears at full volume for decades. We are dancing to the music with gusto. *And it is costing us dearly.*

What I am advocating for in this chapter and in this book is what Sarah Bessey calls "The radical spiritual art of staying put." Later she refers to the "radical act of staying put." She asserts that we have misplaced the sacredness of place. In most of our church traditions, we never hear a word about "the holy work of staying." I'm urging each of us to find our way toward what Eswine calls "a long rhythm in a local place." Eswine continues:

> Because by faith there is more to... these local people with their daily stories, this store-bought or stove-baked bread, and these cups of juice or cheap wine - there is more here, I am saying, than meets the eyes. God is here. *The same old, same old has wings.*

THE CHURCH AS THE FAMILY AT WORSHIP

As I mentioned earlier, however, the church is also a discipleship training school that can and should produce saints. The church is to be a place of personal and spiritual formation. We are formed by the Holy Spirit and by the mutually practiced liturgical habits of the church. In other words, the church will always remain, first and foremost, the gathered body of Christ AT WORSHIP. We exist first to worship God and we are formed by that worship. As Christians, we exist first to gather for worship. That is our core Christian practice. It is intimately related to God's Word. God speaks to us as we hear his word. We then respond and sing and pray God's word back to him ("reversed thunder," as Peterson puts it). We become "Christian" (i.e. Christlike) by praying together as Christians. Christians pray Christian prayers. Christians practice Christian practices. Together. This may seem obvious but it is anything but obvious in the garden variety evangelical churches in my world. At the risk of sounding like a broken record, one of the key formational practices is sticking together. As Sarah Bessey puts it, "***The radical act of staying put is shaping me.***"

I've often defined our church as a "Family of God on a Mission." I recently learned that Pope John Paul II and Pope Benedict XVI defined the church as a "Communio of Disciples in Mission." I like that a lot. Maybe even more than my own definition - because that's how I'm using the word "family." I'm not just saying that it's a close-knit community of people who try to get along with each other and who call each other brother and sister. It's not less than that but it's deeper than that. It's a *communio* (or a communion) created by the Holy Spirit – making it more like a living organism (the body of Christ) than a voluntary society of people who choose to "fellowship" together for a period of time. In that sense, we are more like the cells in a body than like individuals who choose to associate with each other in a volunteer organization (until we move on to another one). Thus, Paul can say to the messed-up bunch in Corinth: "you are the body of Christ and each one of you is a part of it" (I Cor. 12:27).

Don't' misunderstand me. *Family* is obviously still my favorite metaphor for the church. I just want you to know that when I use the word *family,* I'm using it in the sense of a holy *communio* or a living "communion." I also like *Communio of Disciples* because it implies that the church is a community of Christ-followers who are being formed into Christlikeness. And this is done first and foremost by the Holy Spirit - through the formational power of Christian worship (meaning the reading of the word of God, prayer, praise, confession, and most of all, through baptism and the Lord's Supper). This brings us back to worship – the church's primary calling. And one of the unique aspects of worship is that it seems totally useless and impractical to the outside world. That's why we're so often tempted to make our worship services more interesting and attractive and useful and meaningful and, most of all, "*relevant*!" That's also why we need to resist this temptation at all costs and let the church be the church. What the world needs more than anything else is for the church to be the church (and for the church to make the world the world, as Hauerwas would put it). And the church is being the church, at its very best, when it is at worship (and by worship I don't mean sitting as spectators in a large auditorium being entertained by a smokin' hot band (with a fog machine, of course) and a funny interesting speaker in skinny jeans. There's nothing wrong at all with skilled musicians, gifted speakers, or tight jeans. I'm just saying that if that's all it is, worship hasn't even begun yet. By worship, I mean reading the church's scripture and praying the church's prayers. I mean eating and drinking the body and blood of Christ together. As Rachel Held Evans puts it, we need to do the things we've always done and always known to do. Allow me to repeat her words quoted earlier:

> *It's about communion. It's about baptism. It's about confession. It's about healing. It's about death and resurrection and all the beautiful weird things the church has*

always been doing.

One of the best answers to Philip Yancey's question, "Church, Why bother?" is found in Yancey's own reminder that the church does not exist primarily to meet our needs. If the church's main purpose is to worship God then one of the most important reasons to "bother" with gathered worship at church is that it is gloriously impractical and useless. Once again, stay with me. The Catholic theologian, Robert Barron, says it well (*in what may be my favorite quote in this entire book – so read it slowly and carefully*):

> *Aristotle said that the best activities are the most useless. This is because such things are not simply means to a further end but are done entirely for their own sake. Thus, watching a baseball game is more important than getting a haircut, and cultivating a friendship is more valuable than making money. The game and the friendship are goods that are excellent in themselves, while getting a haircut and making money are in service of something beyond themselves. This is also why the most important parts of the newspaper are the sports section and the comics, and not, as we would customarily think, the business and political reports. In this sense, the most useless activity of all is the celebration of the Liturgy, which is another way of saying that it is the most important thing we could possibly do. There is no higher good than to rest*

in God, to honor him for his kindness, to savor his sweetness - in a word, to praise him.

Barron also referred to Guardini's reference to liturgy being "a consummate form of play." Barron explained, "We play football and we play musical instruments because it is simply delightful to do so, and we play in the presence of the Lord for the same reason." Over the years, I've experienced the beauty and the delight of simply gathering with my ordinary church family to rest in God and to give him the honor, praise, and thanksgiving that he is due.

ON PROGRAMS, YOUTH GROUPS, AND "EXCELLENCE"

If you ask my friends and family members, they will tell you that my main weakness as a pastor and leader is my inability to establish and manage the various "programs" of the church. The majority of the criticism directed at me over the years is usually related to this area. Much of the criticism is valid. Part of my problem, however, is a combination of my temperament and my philosophy of ministry. About fifteen years ago, my co-pastors finally demanded that I write my thoughts down on paper. They insisted that I articulate my philosophy of local church ministry - especially as it relates to the various ministry programs in the church. This book actually grew out of that embryonic paper written over fifteen years ago. In this paper, I tried to explain that I actually do love and support all of the various programs of the church. I explained that I had always supported and participated in all of the programs of the church (such as men's ministries, youth ministries, senior citizen ministries, summer camps, and vacation Bible schools, for instance). At the same time, however, I admitted that I always considered them to be *secondary* to our primary identity as members of one church family. Another way to put it: I considered these programs to be very important (and I wish I was better at making sure they survive and thrive - and that they are well run), but even more important (in my humble opinion) is that these young people, men, women, and senior adults discover their primary identity as members of the church family *at large* – as the church family at worship.

To help explain what I mean, I'll include a section from that paper written fifteen years ago. I was using Youth Ministry as my primary illustration. I included a long excerpt from Mike Yaconelli which expressed my heart at the time (and still does). I still consider it to be one of the classic defining texts of my life of ministry. I've left this next section intact in its original form. I urge you to read it carefully. Here's a section from that early paper:

Mike Yaconelli, after 42 years in youth ministry, and after 42 years as one of the nation's leading authorities on ministry to teenagers, wrote an article in *Youthworker Journal* entitled, "A Better Idea Than Youth Ministry." He makes the precise point that I'm attempting to make throughout this book. In his article, Yaconelli wrote that Youth Ministry is a good idea but that the church family is an even better idea. He first affirmed the goodness and the importance of youth ministry: it is relevant to the youth, for example. He called that a good thing. He said that kids can learn about relationships and friendships. He called that good, too. He believed that youth groups could be a safe place where kids could be honest and real. Again, a good thing. He wrote that youth ministry can be truly fun and that that too is a very good thing. He concludes that *youth group is good but there's a better good. It's called church.* He then wrote one of the most beautiful pieces on the church that I've ever read. It speaks my heart and the heart of this book. I wonder if this is where the title, *Ordinary Church*, began to form in my head (I was wrong earlier. This is actually my favorite quote in this entire book. It's quite long but if you read it carefully, you'll pretty much understand my entire philosophy of ministry):

> *Not youth church, or contemporary church, or postmodern church. Just plain, boring, ordinary church. Yes, that's right. Church. The place where people who don't know each other get to know each other; where people who normally don't associate with each other, associate; where people who are different learn how to be one.*

Mostly, church is the place where we can grow old together. And it turns out that growing old together is still the best way to bring lasting results with students. Growing old together is where we teach (and learn from) each other what discipleship means in the everyday world.

I pastor a church that for the last sixteen years hasn't had a youth program (in spite of the fact that I can provide free resources). Nothing. Just church on Sunday morning at ten o'clock where the students had to muddle through a very uncool morning service filled with mistakes, awkward gaps, interruptions, and imperfections. The music? In the language of students...it sucks. We've never had many students in our services, but we've always had some.

And here's the crazy part. The few students we have had over the years? They keep coming back. Most of our students leave town for college or work; but when they are in town they are back in church, usually fighting back the tears. Why?

"It feels like home," they say. "Everyone's so glad to see me. After all these years, I still feel like I belong here. It's like Jesus never left the building."

Somehow, being with a group of diverse people week after week caused a bond to be formed—a family was created, and community happened. The mystery of community became a reality. Community isn't complicated. It's just a group of people who grow old together. They stick with each other through the teenage years, marriage, children, getting old, sick, and finally dying—all the while teaching each other how to follow Christ through the rugged terrain of life.

Maybe the body of Christ is the place where youth ministry was supposed to happen all along.

Twenty years later, those words from the late great Mike Yaconelli still resonate with me and fill my heart with joy. You can imagine, then, how deeply saddened I was when a well-known pastor recently presented the exact opposite approach to youth ministry. To his credit (and I respected him for it), the pastor almost immediately repented and apologized for his insensitive words. We all say crazy things now and then, so my point is not to attack a particular pastor. My point is this: in a nutshell, a well-known pastor called parents who attend ordinary churches "stinkin selfish." He said that if a parent takes their children to a church of "two hundred members," they obviously don't care about their kids. He said that if parents truly cared about their kids, they would make sure that their kids were in a church big enough to have separate middle school and high school groups… so that "kids don't grow up to hate the church." The problem: that's simply not true. My experience over the years has been the exact opposite. The kids who drop out of church and end up hating the church - are often those very kids who are taught from an early age to be self-centered consumers in their relationship to church.

One example comes from a pastor who responded to that pastor's words in this way:

> *I grew up in one of those big ol' megachurches you're talking about, and it taught me to hate church. I would have left in high school if I'd had the option, but in my house, attendance at my cool, hip, contemporary-worshiping, youth-group-glorifying, moralism-preaching, theology-eschewing McCongregation was a non-negotiable. So, I went. Through every repetition of "Shout to the Lord," every True Love Waits commitment ceremony, every rapture-ready dispensationalist Bible study, every sermon series on how to make myself into a good, moral, well-behaved person so that I wouldn't tick off God and bring condemnation to America... I've got a son of my own now, so you'll have to forgive me for being selfish, but as long as I have a say in the matter, he's going to be going to one of those smallish churches where he'll know everyone, and everyone will know him.*

My purpose really isn't to criticize megachurches. It truly isn't. I'm just trying to argue that it's not necessarily the only option, maybe not even the best option. This same pastor who wrote those wise words above responded with a list of counter-instructions called: "Don't take your kids to a megachurch." He wrote, that you should instead:

- **Take your kids to a church that teaches them the true place of corporate worship.** Introduce them to a place where they learn the discipline of liturgy. A place where they reenact the gospel story through Word and Sacrament week in and week out. Take them to a church where they learn the value of stillness and silence, and where there's also grace for them when they fail at it. Take them to a church where they learn to participate, instead of vegging out on jesusy entertainment.

- **Take your kids to a place where they have opportunities to participate in worship.**

- **Take your kids to a church without silos**. Take your kids to a church where they are surrounded by people of all ages who love them and pray for them. Take your kids to a place where their faith is nurtured by mature believers, and where those older saints can be reinvigorated by the beautiful, budding, growing faith of a child. And take them to a place where they learn how to engage with the world around them, so that they can actually be the kingdom people they're called to be.

I've always felt strongly that the worst thing you can do to your children is to teach them to search for a better church – and to pull them out of their own church family at an impressionable age and move them to a church with a better children's program or youth group. Almost certainly, you will plant in them a seed of consumerist Christianity that will set them on a life-long search for churches that "suit them, that fit them, and that feed them." Back when I wrote my Philosophy of Ministry paper, I cited a study that found that over 75% of young people are leaving the church when they become adults. Several recent studies continue to put the percentage at least as high as 66%. Many of these dropouts do return a few years later and most cite simple life change (going to college, for instance) as the main factor, but the fact remains that many don't return. Back when I wrote my paper for my fellow elders, I cited another study that seems to indicate that "this statistic (of youth leaving the church) goes up to the degree that the youth program is large and high-powered. In other words, the 'better' the youth ministry, the higher percentage of dropouts at age eighteen."

I wasn't about to make that mistake so I always made sure we had a lousy youth group! Many of my friends have pointed out that that's the one goal I've successfully reached in my life. That statistic about the "the better the youth group the higher rate of dropout" (if even half true) would make sense, though. If the feeder system of the large youth group is the smaller churches with the "inferior" youth programs (and it is), then the young person is taught a crucial (and destructive) lesson right from the start. They are taught that they are to be religious consumers that shop around for the best religious deal they can find. A few years after they find it, however, they turn eighteen, get kicked out of the exciting group, and are now stuck with regular boring grownup church, so they begin a lifelong search for a good church that fits them. In their twenties, they search for a great "twenty somethings" church, in their thirties a great church for young couples with a couple of kids, and so on and so forth. They spend years as religious consumers until they finally leave the church in selfish boredom. In Phoenix, I'm told that you can find 60-something churches, 70-something churches, and 80-something churches.

OK, I admit, I may have gotten a little carried away. But you can see why I reacted so severely to a pastor accusing the vast majority of us in ordinary churches of "stinkin' selfishness." My experience with my own four children has confirmed my convictions about the "church as family." They always looked forward to going to church and hated to miss out on an opportunity to be with their church family. Why? I got the impression over the years that it was because the church was simply their family. Period. Throughout their lives, they've had friends of all ages in the church. It never crossed their mind to come home and evaluate a program or leader as to whether it was fun enough or exciting enough for their tastes. *Church was just church and it still is... and it's their church. It's their family*. To them, the church is not there to cater to special interest groups – even their own. It's not there to provide attractive programs and services that cater to their needs and tastes. It's really not even there to provide them with good friends and fun experiences. It is what it is, and what it is… is *family – their family.* They learned at an early age that you don't go to church for excitement. As the late great Rich Mullens pointed out, *that's what movies are for. That's what concerts and football games are for. Excitement.* The church, on the other hand, exists to worship God. We gather for fellowship and prayer with people we wouldn't normally hang out with. We gather to learn the apostle's doctrine. We gather to share all things with one another. And, mostly, we gather to exalt God and to proclaim and pray his holy word. The church exists because of God's call. It is none other than the bride of Christ. The body and bride of Christ – at worship, in deep fellowship, and on a mission to love God, to love one another, and to love the world with the love of Christ - *an ordinary family of God at worship and on a mission.*

ON EXCELLENCE

So, is it true that I don't value excellence? I used to think that I didn't. Then I realized, recently, that maybe I do actually care. I just have different priorities. For instance, if you come to my church, I can promise you excellence in the areas of pastoral care, relationships, theology, acceptance, and loyalty, just to name a few things on which I place a premium. When it comes to the programs, performances, and facilities, however, I can't promise a lot of bells and whistles. I can't promise a lot of glitz and glamour. I can't promise things will be hip or cool. I can't even promise great coffee! But I can promise you a loving family with loving shepherds.

HOW TO FIND A GOOD CHURCH

I'll close this chapter by passing on a tidbit of advice from Eugene. In an interview, Jonathan Merritt asked Eugene Peterson if he had any advice for younger Christians who are "itchy for a deeper and more authentic discipleship. Eugene's answer is classic:

> *Go to the nearest smallest church and commit yourself to being there for 6 months. If it doesn't work out, find somewhere else. But don't look for programs, don't look for entertainment, and don't look for a great preacher. A Christian congregation is not a glamorous place, not a romantic place. That's what I always told people. If people were leaving my congregation to go to another place of work, I'd say, "Find the smallest church, the closest church, and stay there for 6 months." Sometimes it doesn't work. Some pastors are just incompetent. And some are flat out bad. So, I don't think that's the answer to everything, but it's a better place to start than going to the one with all the programs, the glitz, all that stuff.*

CHAPTER SEVEN

First Church of the Individual

"The tune of radical individualism has been playing in our ears at full volume for decades. We are dancing to the music with gusto. And it is costing us dearly."

– *Joseph Hellerman*

"Do you despise the church?" This is the angry question asked by the Apostle Paul to his former congregation at First Church Corinth (I Cor. 11:22). Another translation: "Do you show contempt for the church?" Paul may very well want to address this question to many American Christians in our day. This contempt for the community has been around for thousands of years and is alive and well today. From the beginning of time, it seems that anti-communal individualism has always been a major temptation for the people of God, and for human beings in general. We may, however, be living in the most community-despising, hyper-individualistic time in human history (so far, at least). There are many major studies that discuss the current state of western civilization. The works of Charles Taylor (*A Secular Age*), Alasdair MacIntyre (*After Virtue*), and Christian Smith and Melinda Denton (*Soul Searching: The Religious and Spiritual Lives of American Teenagers)* are examples of some of the significant works of our generation. These types of books and several others are discussed and summarized in Rod Dreher's recent book, *The Benedict Option*. One of the many things he draws from these various studies on our current cultural condition, is that we are suffering from a serious form of hyper-individualism.

For many centuries, the individual seemed to get pushed aside in favor of the community. In the last few centuries, the pendulum has swung in the other direction. Individual rights and individualism have come to dominate the thinking of most people and the needs of the community have been pushed aside. In the broader scope of world history, there are many good and noble consequences of this enlightened pendulum swing towards individualism. Human beings have experienced great advances in the area of individual rights, dignity, and freedom. In the church world within modern American society, however, we seem to now suffer from the opposite problem: hyper-individualism. The pendulum seems to have swung too far. Individualism, taken to its logical extreme can also be ugly.

FIRST CHURCH OF ELEUSIS REVISITED

There was a famous religious shrine in the ancient world at a place called *Eleusis*. For a thousand years, from around 600 B.C.E until 395 C.E., countless people visited this shrine hoping to obtain salvation, inner transformation, renewed strength, increased happiness, and even the promise of a happy afterlife. These benefits were promised to each individual who visited the shrine - that is, the blessings were offered and received entirely *individually*. There were no social elements or social consequences attached to these spiritual gifts. According to New Testament scholar Gerhard Lohfink, men and women from all over the Roman Empire - even Roman emperors - came to Eleusis in search of these benefits. They came for over a thousand years until the shrine was destroyed by Christianized Goths under King Alaric in the year 395 C.E. Gerhard Lohfink, in his marvelous book, *Does God Need the Church*, provides great insight into viewing Eleusis as a model of individualistic salvation.

Eleusis does indeed serve as a powerful model for the personal, individual quest to achieve salvation - which is the dominant religious model in our culture today. In the end, in themselves, the religious celebrations at Eleusis were nearly the opposite of the New Testament concept of Christian community.
At Eleusis, the individual alone receives salvation. Eleusis

knew absolutely nothing of the building up of congregations or churches. The person who experienced the mysteries of Eleusis and participated in the ceremony of personal salvation immediately returned to their daily lives without any new ties or restrictions. If you're familiar with American Christianity, this should sound quite familiar to you. Think about it:

SALVATION AND SPIRITUALITY IN ANCIENT ELEUSIS:

- **Salvation with "no strings attached."**
- **Salvation with no social consequences.**
- **Salvation without any necessary creeds or beliefs.**
- **Salvation with no congregation or church.**
- **Salvation without any social or relational expectations or requirements of any kind.**
- **Salvation without any guilt-trips or pressure.**
- **Salvation without any accountability.**
- **Salvation that is completely personal and individual.**
- **Salvation through a person's own personal spiritual experience.**
- **Salvation that is private and nobody else's business.**

I contend that we American Christians are immersed in a similar kind of hyper-individualism and consumerism like we saw in ancient Eleusis. I contend that popular American spirituality could be called "Eleusis Revisited" or "Eleusis 2.0."

It's what you hear constantly on T.V. and in radio interviews. And it has seeped into the church and shaped our common faith and practice. Christianity in America, at the popular level, is often a baptized version of this same Eleusis-type spirituality - Eluesis 2.0 with a Christian fish and an American flag. The American religion is a rival religion, a civil religion made up of a hodgepodge collection of nationalism and a vague Eleusis style spirituality with a little Christian seasoning sprinkled on top. *America's religion is America.* The American church is all tangled up in red, white, and blue (to quote a phrase from Brian Zahnd). And since most Christians are first Americans, and secondly Christians, that means that most American Christians are, first and foremost, hard core individualist consumers.

Let me explain how this modern American version of *Eleusis* works itself out in everyday life. Many American Christians are not bothered by haphazard church attendance. Many are far more bothered, for instance, by a professional football player who doesn't stand during the national anthem than they are by a Christian who doesn't stand up and worship Christ on the Lord's Day (*every Lord's Day*). In other words, it doesn't seem to bother most American Christians if they miss church – for whatever reason. Worse than that, it doesn't bother tens of millions of American Christians if they go to church at all. But they are outraged if they see someone skip the national anthem before a football game. Similarly, I know of many fellow Christians who would be more offended by removing an American flag from a sanctuary than they would be by the removal of a cross. I know of other Christians who are more passionate about their Second Amendment gun rights than they are about their First Amendment rights to freely worship each week. They are much more passionately committed to the values of the National Rifle Association than they are to the values presented in the Sermon on the Mount. By the way, one way to tell if you've got your priorities a bit messed up: you're a little offended right this very minute because I mentioned the flag, the national anthem, and the NRA. I'm not actually criticizing those things. I'm comparing them to Lord's Day worship, the Kingdom of God, and the Sermon on the Mount – and there should be no comparison.

Another evidence of consumerist Christianity is that many Christians think it's more important to find a church that has more attractive "bells and whistles" for their children than it is for their children to grow up in their own church family, i.e. to go *together through life* with their lifelong friends and relatives.

Another example is how rarely one of us would choose the location of our family home based on the location of our church home. Almost always, we choose our homes based mostly on how much home we can get for our money, the quality of the neighborhood, possibly the academic rating of the schools, and maybe a few other factors. But, rarely if ever, do I encounter Christians who choose their home based on how it will affect their participation in their home congregation. This would be consistent with the thesis of this book: we don't typically place a high value on our local congregation and its central role in our life of faith. I've witnessed, in a few cases, where families have been adversely affected – possibly for generations – by suddenly removing their children from their home congregation.

Conversely, you can understand why I was so moved by the testimony of Rod Dreher in his book, *The Benedict Option*, a book I mentioned earlier. One of its strengths, again, is its high view of the local church. Dreher tells the story of how he and his family moved back to his small hometown in Louisiana to be near his sister, Ruthie, who was stricken with terminal cancer. When he returned home, he was struck by the depth and stability he saw in Ruthie's life. She had remained in that small town her entire life and was surrounded and supported by a deep network of friends and relatives – who cared for her and her husband and her children during her nineteen-month struggle and even after her passing. Dreher saw a real-life example of St. Benedict's rule of "stability." Dreher (and St. Benedict) knew that there are exceptions. Not everyone is called to stay in their hometown or return to it later in life. But, barring unusual circumstances, St. Benedict's wisdom was that "if you are going to put down spiritual roots, you need to stay in one place long enough for them to go deep." As Dreher put it, "not everyone is called to return to their hometown, of course, but everybody should think deeply about the spiritual and emotional costs" of moving around freely for financial or vocational success.

When Rod Dreher and his family returned to their hometown they realized the life-and-death importance of having a home church. As soon as possible, they became part of a young Eastern Orthodox church. Four years later, when that fledgling church had to close down, Dreher and his wife came to an amazing counter-cultural conclusion:

> *...my wife and I took stock of how much we and our children had grown in faith and discipleship from four years of praying communally and liturgically with our congregation. We decided that we could not be without an Orthodox parish nearby, so we could be there at every opportunity. That's one reason why we packed up our things and moved to Baton Rouge, forty-five minutes away. We knew that there would be no way to practice our faith properly in community while living so far from the church.*

Did you catch that? Can you imagine anything more un-American? Dreher and his family moved forty-five minutes away in order to be closer to their home church! How rare it is to see anyone making proximity to one's home church a major factor in choosing a home. Dreher goes on to say something that is the thesis of this book:

> *Why be close? Because, as I said earlier, the church can't just be the place you go on Sundays – it must become the center of your life.*

Amen, amen, and a thousand amens. My dream and my prayer are that we would move towards making church a priority, towards this vision of community, and away from the cultural bondage of hyper-individualism and hyper-consumerism. We must declare war on the individualized, privatized version of spirituality and salvation that is so ubiquitous in American culture. The Christian church's best theologians, saints, and pastors have always distinguished true Christian faith from a gnostic, ethereal "no strings attached, no accountability, no community, Eleusian-type" pseudo-spirituality. We must remain diligent in doing the same.

Examples of "First Church of the Individual" abound in popular music, movies, media, and literature. One recent one is the popular country song by Maren Morris called "My Church," in which the chorus ends with the words:

> *When I play the highway FM*
> *I find my soul revival*
> *Singing every single verse*

Yeah I guess that's my church

Maren is a talented artist and the song is certainly a catchy tune. I get her point. But the song's message is nothing more than a cliché we've heard all our lives. All my life I've heard people say, "the mountains are my church," "the golf course is my church," "I feel closest to God when I'm working in my garden – that's my church," or "my church is at home watching a worship service on television," and hundreds of variations on this theme. So, when Maren Morris declares that driving around listening to the radio is "her church," it's hardly a revolutionary idea. She says that when she listens to Hank Williams and Johnny Cash on the radio, it feels like a spiritual experience and that constitutes church for her.

Believe me when I say that I, too, love Hank Williams and Johnny Cash. They are among my favorites. Like Maren Morris, I also love to drive down the road listening to them. At times, I, too, have had what you could call a religious experience driving down the road listening to good music. I, too, have spent my life in the high mountains sensing God's presence there in special and unique ways. My point is that it is never either/or. You don't have to choose between these wonderful experiences and a true church home. You can drive down the road and enjoy Williams and Cash. You can spend hours in your garden and enjoy God's presence. You can sit on a beach or ski down a mountain and feel close to God.

You can even enjoy a worship service on television (although this one should come with warning labels). But none of these experiences constitute "church." They may be wonderful experiences but they are *not* church. They may make you feel good, but you never have to replace your church with them. I remember Pastor Kindschy telling me that parishioners would tell him, "I worship God better on the golf course." He would always tell me, "the problem is, we don't end up worshipping God on the golf course." He then would add, "Take this to the bank, Joe. Without a single exception, every time someone begins to drift away from regular church attendance, they drift away from Jesus. I've never seen an exception in eighty years."

Sometimes a person will say, "God never commands us to go to church!" Well, that's not quite accurate. For one, the biblical authors *assume* you're already at church! The New Testament apostles assume that you are reading their letters which were written for Christians to hear *at church!* Naturally, they don't have to explicitly and frequently command a Christian to go to church. That would be like someone writing a love letter to the love of their life and commanding them over and over in the letter to sit down and carefully read. Frank Sheed, in his book, *Theology and Sanity,* reminds us that Christ did not just leave it up to his followers to decide if they wanted to form their own little groups *if it seemed good to them* or if they wanted to remain isolated *if it seemed good to them.* No! Jesus "banded them into a flock, a society, a church." It reminds me of the popular comment, "Jesus didn't come to start a new religion." Of course not. He already had one. Jesus is described as a very religious person in countless places (like in Luke 4:16), with words like: "on the Sabbath day Jesus went into the synagogue, *as was his custom*." Jesus was the fulfillment of the Old Covenant in every way. He then expanded, reconstituted, and transformed the covenant people of God into the New Covenant people. But the New Covenant people were no less religious than the Old Covenant people – if by religious you mean a people that gathers regularly and officially to pray, fellowship, give offerings, sing songs, hear the Scriptures read and expounded upon, etc. Sounds a lot like church, doesn't it? We're right back where we began with grandma telling us to go to church.

Jason Swan Clark, in a recent blog entitled "You Don't Need to Go to Church to be a Christian and other fairy tales," discussed the tendency of American Christians to come up with excuses as to why they don't need to attend church every week:

> *The internal stories are often these: 'I need a break, I need to focus on my kids/family, I want time to myself, I have to get this marathon/triathlon/course done', etc. We then succumb to, and placate, any doubts we might have about our stories with more fabrications. 'I can get back to church later', 'it won't affect me', and, even worse, 'this is what's best for me'. Such stories are,*

> *at best, fantasies, fairy tales and myths. At worst, they are mendacities that destroy God's work in us and the world. Satan is indeed the father of lies, prowling around looking to devour us. His greatest ploy and tactic has not been a full-frontal assault on belief; instead it has been the insidious entropy of attendance. A lion secures its prey by first isolating it, so it is then free to devour it.... The lie of not going to church is the most destructive and isolating falsity of all.*

"My Church." As a Christian, I don't get to decide what "my church" is. This attitude of choosing and designing "my own church" (or my own spirituality or my own "god") is very Eleusian – which is to say very American. As a Christian, all that matters is the church that Jesus Christ is building. Christ proclaimed, "I will build *my church* and the gates of hades shall not prevail against it." The church is not mine. In that sense, only Jesus gets to call the church "my church." Neither Marin Morris, nor you, nor I, get to define "my church." The church is the body of Christ and a creation of the Holy Spirit. I get invited *into* the church – which already exists. The church is not something that I get to make up. The church is something that already existed for thousands of years - into which I am incorporated. I have no desire to criticize Maren Morris at all. Her catchy tune is simply an example of the cultural milieu in which we all live and breathe. It reveals the shallow and self-centered way in which we view the church, spirituality, and salvation. We are truly Eleusis 2.0. My point is this: the church is something into which we are called. We are members of one body and we belong to each other. "My church" is not just anywhere I happen to feel good or where I happen to feel free or feel saved. It is an official community into which the Holy Spirit places me. It is a place where I am called to gather to worship God and to serve others. The church is not first and foremost *about* me or *for* me. Although, ironically, as a side benefit of serving and worshiping, the church turns out to be the only way towards true health and happiness (or, at least, a primary way) – and the place where I am best formed as a Christ-follower.

Hopefully, you recall what constitutes a church. The whole point of an actual church is that it is filled with people "unlike" me. If you avoid going to a church, for instance, because there are too many conservatives in that congregation (or too many liberals or too many rich folk, poor folk, rednecks, extroverts, introverts or just too many people of a different race or culture…) then you're missing the whole point of church. Remember, the church is *by design* a community of "differents" (to quote Scot McKnight again). Remember, the church is not about you and is intended *by design* to bring together people who would not normally associate with each other. In the "Big Book" of Alcoholics Anonymous there is the statement,

> *We are a people who normally would not mix. But*

> *there is a fellowship… and an understanding which is indescribably wonderful. We are like the passengers of a great liner the moment after the rescue from shipwreck.*

Recovering alcoholics are describing a community of "differents" – people totally unlike one another in almost every way – who share a common bond because of something deeper than all their differences. They suffered a common fate, they shared a narrow escape from certain death, and they now share a common salvation. They don't have the luxury of defining and creating "my fellowship." In the same way, we don't get to define and create "my church." I have to accept everyone Jesus accepts into this common fellowship. I don't get to have Jesus without his friends – and, apparently, Jesus has very low standards when it comes to his friends. That is the constant reminder given to us by Eugene Peterson. Over and over he reminds us that the church is not "ideal." It is not, nor was it ever intended to be, a gathering of nice respectable people. "God is not fastidious in the company he keeps," Peterson writes. If you want to find Jesus, you will find him in the ordinary places. If you want to find the way to true spiritual maturity, you will find it through the commonplace – and rarely in the grandiose, intoxicating, ecstatic, sensational times and places.

Another relevant example (of the Eleusian nature of modern Christianity in America) comes from William Willimon. He tells the story of being at a souvenir store in Egypt. The store's owner suddenly shut the store down right in the middle of the morning with the store full of shoppers. Why? It was prayer time (the owner was Muslim). Can you imagine an American Christian doing this? Can you imagine any of us Christians shutting down our business in order to pray? Can you imagine one of us doing this on a Sunday? Can you imagine us being strict with our schedules on a Sunday morning and saying to a friend, a visiting relative, a coach, or a boss that our gathered worship is basically non-negotiable? Just for fun, I've thought up a few statements we're not likely to hear from fellow Christians:

- *"oh, I'm sorry. I worship God on Sunday mornings from ten to noon. You're welcome to come with me or to stay home - but that's when we pray."*

- *"Oh, I'm sorry, I can't get there until afternoon. We worship and pray until noon."*

- *"Oh, I'm sorry – little Johnny can play or practice any time during the other 166 hours of the week. But we worship God from ten to noon every Sunday morning."*

- *"No, I'm sorry. We can't have that brunch for grandma until a little after noon. Before that, we worship and pray."*

- *"I do need a job badly and I'd love to work here. But I do have one request. I worship God every Sunday morning from ten until noon. I'm willing to work any other time of the week and I'll be very reliable and hard working. Just not during those two hours. That's when I worship and pray."*

- *"Is there a flight departing later on Sunday so I don't miss Sunday worship?"*

- *"Is there a way I could return late Saturday night so I don't miss worship on Sunday?"*

Now, please remember, I'm not as legalistic as I sound. I know that there are exceptions and variations. I know that some people have to work on Sundays (doctors and police, for example). I know that some people worship at different times or on different days. I also know that there are occasions where we just can't or won't make it to the worship service. My point is how rare it is that we even think in these ways.

The church in America is not under attack... It's under neglect.

Many of the people who are fighting the culture war online could do far better by throwing that time and energy into supporting their local church. The problem in our country is not that *they* took prayer out of the public schools. Our problem is that *we* took prayer out of the church (sometimes by dropping out altogether and joining the post-church crowd, other times by just dropping in and out of church now and then). The problem isn't that *they* are trying to take away our Second Amendment rights. The problem is that *we* aren't exercising our First Amendment rights to worship regularly and faithfully in our home church. The problem in this country is not football players who won't honor the National Anthem. The problem is Christians who won't honor the anthem of heaven, the song of the redeemed - with Christians they wouldn't normally associate with – as part of the body of Christ, the bride of Christ, the church. And, once again, you and I don't get to invent the church, make up the church, define or create the church. We don't get to decide what is or is not "my church." Our only choice is whether or not to accept the invitation.

CHAPTER EIGHT

The Patient Ferment of the Ordinary Church

"Church growth strategies are the death gurgle of a church that has lost its way."

- Stanley Hauerwas

Obviously, this chapter's title is a takeoff on Alan Kreider's remarkable book, *The Patient Ferment of the Early Church*. Kreider beautifully demonstrates that the genius behind the early church's healthy growth was her patient commitment to simply *being* the church – nothing more, nothing less. According to Kreider, you could also put it the other way around: *their commitment to patience was the cardinal virtue of the early church's witness*. Or, as John Howard Yoder put it, "The key to the obedience of God's people is not their effectiveness but their patience." During the first few centuries of the church's unfathomable survival and growth, the Christian communities showed almost zero interest in "immediate results." They showed no interest in what we would call evangelism programs. Most of all, there wasn't the slightest hint of an effort to attract outsiders to their worship gatherings. In other words, there was no hint of a *seeker sensitive* or *attractional* approach.

I call your attention, again, to the message of Rachel Held Evans when she pointed out that the Christian church already knows what to do and what to be. The church's calling is to do the things she has always done and to be what she has always been (word, sacrament, liturgy, Holy Communion, baptism, fellowship, praise, prayer). The church should remain weird to the surrounding secular and pagan culture. She should remain weird in the eyes of the rival religion of Americanism. The church, in a word, should look uncomfortably "ordinary." Alan Kreider argues convincingly that the *key* to early Christianity's shocking growth was ordinary Christians who were formed in ordinary congregations which formed the center of their lives. He writes,

> *The Christian assembly was not one of a palette of social commitments of an urban Roman; it was the center of the Christians' lives. It was not one aspect of a varied religious life; it was their religious life... This had enormous formative power.*

These ordinary Christians would then "continue the ferment" that had begun in these close-knit church families, and as they traveled and worked, they spread the faith. In other words, what was so wildly *attractive* to outsiders in the first few centuries were *not* the churches or their services, events, buildings, or programs. Instead, it was the Christians themselves that were so attractive. But these Christians became so attractive as they were deeply formed and transformed by their regular and loyal participation in their home congregation, (which was their "first family" – their brothers and sisters in the faith). And these churches were marked by an amazing *patience* to simply be themselves – without any concern whatsoever about immediate results. They were patient enough to simply worship Jesus together and make disciples - *one at a time if necessary* - no matter how long it took. They were patient enough to simply pray and sing and read and teach and share meals together – sharing in Holy Communion and baptizing people into Christ – and trusting God to work it all out in his way and in his time. There were no business strategies, no vision statements, no five-year plans, no leadership conferences, and no marketing plans. Just ordinary local congregations - patient enough to trust God to cause his church to ferment, grow, survive, and thrive – in God's way, in God's power, and in God's time.

Stanley Hauerwas and William Willimon (in *Resident Aliens*, for instance), teach us that the church's primary calling is for *the church to be the church.* And when the church is the church, it is a family of God – a congregation - that worships Jesus, knows Jesus, and follows Jesus. It may be more than that, but it is never less than that. I don't even mind if you use the beautiful phrase: "simply Jesus" or merely Jesus. But, never forget that to be simply with Jesus is to be simply with him *together*. We follow Jesus *together through life*, or we do not follow him at all. In the words of Pastor Brian Zahnd:

> *Salvation is a kind of belonging... if the Jesus we follow doesn't lead us into the community of other followers, we are following a mostly made-up Jesus, a manufactured Jesus designed to accommodate the modern cult of "me."*

- So, Rachel would put it this way: *the church already knows what to do.*
- Hauerwas and Willimon would say it this way: *the church's highest calling is always to simply be the church.*
- Eugene Peterson would say it this way*: the church needs to follow Jesus in the Jesus Way.*
- Peterson would confirm that the Jesus way is the way of patience: "*A long obedience in the same direction.*"

Maybe this is a good place for a heavy dose of Eugene Peterson at his best:

> *We have a huge advertising industry designed to stir up appetites we didn't even know we had. We are insatiable. It didn't take long for some of our colleagues to develop consumer congregations. If we have a nation*

> *of consumers, obviously the quickest and most effective way to get them into our churches is to identify what they want and offer it to them. Satisfy their fantasies, promise them the moon, recast the gospel into consumer terms — entertainment, satisfaction, excitement and adventure, problem-solving, whatever. We are the world's champion consumers, so why shouldn't we have state-of-the-art consumer churches? There's only one thing wrong. This is not the way that God brings us into conformity with the life of Christ. This is not the way that we become less and Jesus becomes more. This is not the way in which our lives become available to others in justice and service. The cultivation of consumer spirituality is the antithesis of a sacrificial, "denying yourself" congregation.* ***A consumer church is an anti-Christ church.*** *It's doing the right thing—gathering a congregation—but doing it in the wrong way.*

It is so counter-intuitive, so counter-cultural, to say that the Christian church grew most rapidly and most powerfully when the church was most notably *not* in a hurry. It did this against all odds. In one sense, we shouldn't be surprised. Jesus Christ promised that he would build his church and that all the powers of Hades would not thwart Christ's project. And then that same Lord Jesus told the church how to go about its business in the face of opposition, tribulation, and persecution. In his letters to the early churches (the book of *Revelation*), Jesus (through John) praises one of the churches because they kept his command to *"endure patiently."* Throughout the book, all of which is a message to the early church on how to go about its business as resident aliens in "Babylon," the word of God is clear:

"This calls for *patient endurance* and *faithfulness* on the part of God's People." (Rev. 13:10)

"This calls for *patient endurance* on the part of the people of God who keep his commands and remain *faithful* to Jesus." (Rev. 14:12)

How is it that we missed these clear directives? How is it that our modern way of doing church is almost completely devoid of this emphasis on patience? God's word is clear: when the church is going through tough times, turbulent waters, trials and tribulations (which is all the time), the church is called to a deep and profound *patience*. Hence, the patient ferment of the ordinary church was the God-ordained way of the early church and remains the way forward in the twenty-first century.

SLOW CHURCH

C. Christopher Smith and John Pattison have given us all a special gift with their insightful book, *Slow Church: Cultivating Community in the Patient Way of Jesus.* Smith and

Pattison make a compelling case that the Christian church in America should do everything in its power to resist "the cult of speed" (Carl Honore's description) so prevalent in our culture. They draw our attention to Honore, a Canadian journalist, who writes that "fast" and "slow" are more than just different rates of change – they are ways of being or philosophies of life. According to Honore,

FAST *is:*

busy, controlling, aggressive, hurried, analytical, stressed, superficial, impatient, active, quantity-over-quality.

Slowly read those words again and I dare you to not see them as accurate descriptions of our modern way of doing church. On the other hand,

SLOW is:

Calm, careful, receptive, still, intuitive, unhurried, patient, reflective, quality-over-quantity

Now, slowly re-read these words and I dare you not to see them as describing the way of Jesus and the patient way of the early church. Smith and Pattison make a compelling case that the slow and patient way is still the best way. It's the way of Jesus in my opinion. It's the way envisioned by Eugene Peterson, and it's the way I'm attempting to describe throughout this book. The slow and patient way is the exact opposite way of the fast and impatient way. The popular way of doing church in America is much more similar, for instance, to the fast food industry. Years ago, in that long "Philosophy of Ministry" paper I wrote for my fellow elders, I went on an extended rant comparing the church growth movement to the fast food industry. I called the section "*Would You Like Fries With That*?" Some of it is a bit dated, but here's the entire section for your enjoyment:

WOULD YOU LIKE FRIES WITH THAT?

I believe that there is an uncanny resemblance between the modern American church and the fast-food industry. Brennan Manning says it well, "The fast-food culture of this country is an apt metaphor for the state of the church. We're overfed and undernourished, both physically and spiritually." I recently finished reading a book called *Fast Food Nation* by Eric Schlosser. I was startled – and saddened – by the remarkable resemblance between how the fast food industry thinks and how the church growth "experts" think. Schlosser wrote, for instance, about the fast food industry's focus on attracting children. Children are viewed as "surrogate salesmen" who are expected to persuade their parents to take them to McDonald's. A manufacturer of "playlands" explains why fast food operators build them: "Playlands bring in children, who bring in parents, who bring in money." I've heard pastors say the same thing. The basic thinking behind fast food is basically the same thinking underlying the church growth movement: endorse the culture's values, especially the values of quick, easy, convenient, and uniform. You must cater to the customer's "felt needs," present yourself as a "trusted friend" who cares and, by all means, communicate professionalism, cleanliness, and safety. The same kind of thinking that has wiped out small businesses, obliterated regional differences, and spread identical stores throughout the country is the same kind of thinking that has permeated the American church. Almost every facet of American life has now been franchised or chained. The key concept in the fast food industry is *uniformity*. As I visit churches around the country, I am seeing more and more "uniformity" in the church world as well. It seems as if everybody is singing the same songs in the same way, preaching with the same style, and building the same kinds of buildings in the same kinds of neighborhoods, using the same marketing approaches. We've apparently discovered some principles, tools, and techniques that work well. It's one thing, however, for Wal-Mart and McDonald's to run off all of the small "mom & pop" grocery stores and cafes… but it's an entirely different matter when the religious Wal-Marts and the giant McChurches run off the ordinary churches. I have a hard time believing that God is pleased.

I find it very interesting and, I guess, sadly amusing, that several churches have now opened McDonald's restaurants on their property or, in some cases, inside the church building itself. Now you can get your religion and your food at the same place in pretty much the same way and for the same reasons. The values and attitudes that drive McDonald's drive the modern American church. We might as well share the same property. Eric Schlosser's concluding plea regarding the fast food industry could be applied almost word-for-word to the modern church growth movement (let him who has ears to hear hear):

> *Future historians, I hope, will consider the American fast food industry a relic of the twentieth century – a set of attitudes, systems, and beliefs that emerged from postwar southern California, that embodied its limitless faith in technology, that quickly spread across the globe, flourished briefly, and then receded, once its true costs became clear and its thinking became obsolete... Whatever replaces the fast food industry should be regional, diverse, authentic, unpredictable, sustainable ...and humble. It should know its limits. People can be fed without being fattened or deceived. This new century may bring an impatience with conformity, a refusal to be kept in the dark, less greed, more compassion, less speed, more common sense, a sense of humor about brand essences and loyalties, a view of food as more than just fuel. Things don't have to be the way they are. Despite all evidence to the contrary, I remain optimistic.*

Brian D. McLaren, in his classic book, *A New Kind of Christian,* provided us with another relevant quote. He puts these words into the mouth of "NEO:"

> *One of the ways modernity captured Christianity was in this area of mission... We became purveyors of religious goods and services, seeking a clientele, competing for market share, complete with brand names and all the rest. If you want useful plastic kitchen articles, you go to Wal-Mart. If you want low-cost, high-fat food in generous portions, you go to Taco Bell. If you want a standard, scripted vacation, you go to Disney World. If you want a fizzy, sugary drink, you go to Coca-Cola. And if you want a spiritual pick-me-up, you go to church. This put us in a situation exactly opposite to – as I see it – Christ's intent.*

This slow and patient way of early church life is the way that Smith and Pattison envision in their book. Their proposal is a way of "reimagining what it means to be communities of believers gathered and rooted in particular places at a particular time." They seek to help us "unmask and repent of our industrialized and McDonaldized approaches to church." They suggest that the sacrificial way of Jesus just might be calling us to forsake the supersized life. They even go so far as to suggest that we consider praying the "reverse prayer of Jabez:"

God, shrink our territory, and narrow our boundaries
That we might truly be a blessing to all.

THE GOSPEL ACCORDING TO WENDELL BERRY

As I said, the slow and patient church is the kind of church that is described in the life and ministry of Eugene Peterson. It is also the kind of church that would fit the main themes of Wendell Berry's life work. If you want to more fully understand what I mean by "slow church" vs. "fast church," I encourage you to read Wendell Berry. It's similar to his contrast between "Agriculture" and "Agribusiness." My all-time favorite novel is Berry's *Jayber Crow*. In all of Berry's books, both fiction and non-fiction, his main theme is the sacredness of *place*, the holiness of *locale*. Like Eugene Peterson, Berry hammers home the truth that there is glory in the ordinary and that there is beauty and dignity in the local – in a local community, a local environment, a local culture, and in a local farmer's life work. I've often compared pastoral work to farm work. Both are slow, repetitive, careful, and attentive. Both are extremely context specific. Both are uniquely tailored to the unique conditions of soil and water in that particular place.

The first thing my Grandpa Beach did when he arrived in the Central Valley of California, was to work for a winemaker in his vineyards (Cribari Wines). He worked long hard days, saved his money, and finally bought a section of the farm from Mr. Cribari. He became the owner of the "Beach Ranch." Patience is required to be a good pastor in the same way patience is required of a good winemaker. An authentic winemaker knows that they don't really "make" wine. As they say, "we simply prepare the environment for wine to come into being." In the same way, good pastors prepare the environment for disciples to come into being and then wait for God to create them. Authentic disciples are made in the same way as authentic wines. And what confers authenticity in disciples and wines are the same things: a rootedness in family, a local tradition, unique soil conditions, a local culture and the connectedness between them all. You can push out mass-produced and mass-marketed wines and churches in much the same way: where all the wines and churches look, taste, and smell the same and "aren't from anywhere." You just follow a formula and out pops "the product that sells." The problem is: we don't need wines and churches that merely "sell." As Terry Theiese puts it, we need wines [and churches] that have birth certificates. In other words, they are "from somewhere" and not all alike. They come from a unique family with a unique history. They are grounded. Terry Theiese continues, talking about wine (but he could be talking about ordinary churches just as well), "they are more artisanal, more intimately scaled, humbler, and less likely to be blown about by the ephemeral breezes of fashion." This is the gospel according to Wendell Berry and Eugene Peterson and Terry Theiese:

The smartest thing a cellarmaster [or pastor] can know is the right time… to do nothing.

I grew up on my grandfather's farm (actually we called it an orange ranch) and I'm familiar with the daily and annual rhythms of the farmer's life. As I began my life as a pastor, I recognized the similarities between my grandfather and Pastor Kindschy. I also learned early on in ministry that many men and women simply aren't cut out to be local church pastors – for the same reasons they aren't cut out to be farmers. They are too impatient. That's why Eugene Peterson refers to impatience as the besetting sin of pastors. It may be the besetting sin of most American Christians these days. If you asked me to describe the fundamental difference between the modern church and the early church, I'd put it this way:

The Patient Ferment of the Early Church
Vs.
The Impatient Stagnation of the Modern Church

The impatient modern pastor (and congregation) seeks programs and techniques that work well and that work well *right now!* The one thing he or she will avoid at all costs is patient dependence on factors beyond their control. To them, what's intolerable is not knowing exactly what to do or where to go. The thought of waiting, waiting, waiting… for a crop to mature, for a field to lay fallow for a season, for a wounded tree to recover, for a young orchard to produce, for the drought to end… drives the modern pastor (and congregation) crazy. Wendell Berry, on the other hand, says that that's just when the fun starts. In one of his well-known poems, he writes, *It may be that when we no longer know what to do / we have come to our real work / and when we no longer know which way to go / we have begun our real journey*. When I read those words, I couldn't help but think of how blessed I have been to witness Pastor Kindschy's deep wisdom and Christlike patience as he served as a faithful shepherd and as I served as his lucky apprentice, day after day, decade after decade. As Wendell Berry continued, *The mind that is not baffled is not employed / The impeded stream is the one that sings.*

THE LESSON OF ST. LAVAUGHN

The story of our long-time former church secretary, LaVaughn Gillespie, is another wonderful example of the beauty and power of a slow and patient *ordinary church*. LaVaughn went on to her heavenly reward in 2017 after a life filled with many painful losses. Growing up, she lost several family members to death. Finally, she lost her husband while she was still in her forties. She then raised her children alone and walked and prayed as a faithful widow for the next forty-two years. One time, her daughter was near death in the hospital. During her later years, she discovered her beloved grandson after he had taken his own life in LaVaughn's own home. Throughout her years of faithful service, she served as our wonderful church secretary. She was so steady, so wise, and so faithful that she became a true saint in our eyes. She earned this reputation, as I explained at her funeral:

> *Our dear sister Gillespie rightly earned that title of saint. It came by the grace and power of God, yes. But it also came through a life of suffering. More than any of us ever knew, the theme that ran through her life, from beginning to end, was the loss and death of her loved ones. She received a high and holy calling: a life of loneliness and loss like few people ever experienced. And yet for 88 years, she answered that call and walked that lonely road with amazing joy and love and steady faith. Her vision of God, her gaze upon her Savior and Lord never wavered. When she said that the Lord was her refuge and her strength, she meant it. She lived that daily. When she said that the Lord was her shepherd leading her beside quiet waters, she meant it.*

Here's what I want to say, though: For around a decade or so (from around 2000 -2010), other pastors wondered why we didn't get a new secretary. When they heard that LaVaughn didn't use a computer and still did all of our church books by hand, they questioned our sanity. Her hearing began to fail so she didn't like to answer the church phone. I had to prepare the bulletin myself on the computer so that she could then make copies of it. Other pastors would look at us like we were from a different planet. But I always answered the same way: “At Amazing Grace Church, we care more about people like LaVaughn than we do about office efficiency or professional polish. She remains a huge blessing to us and to our church. Her gifts and her faithful service mean more to us than speed and professional excellence. *People over programs!* People over the machine of the organization. Every time.” Besides, it’s not like we suffered at all. She worked hard, she did an excellent job, our books were kept meticulously and accurately, she was as faithful and trustworthy as a person could be. Eventually, she did retire and we hired her successor - another woman from the congregation who exhibited many of the same qualities and traits as St. LaVaughn. My point is this: this is just one example of how a slow and patient church might do its business.

We had a similar experience when our wonderful maintenance man, Mike Woodford, was diagnosed with Alzheimer’s disease not long after we hired him. We started seeing some red flags when he would buy the same tool three times or go next door and forget why he was there. Because we put people over program, it’s was just instinctual for us to take our time with Mike in helping him make the transition out of his working life. We worked with his family and made sure they knew that the process could take as long as it needs to take. We weren’t in a hurry.

Another common mark of a slow and patient church is *decision making by consensus*. Amazing Grace Church has always been governed by an elder board consisting of co-equal pastors who make decisions by consensus. This process which consists of discussion and prayer until a consensus is reached among the elders – can be painfully slow and frustrating. From a business standpoint, it doesn't work very well. But, in another sense, it's worked well. There's never been a church split or fight in sixty-three years. That doesn't mean that people haven't left disgruntled – many have come and gone over the years. But it does mean that the body has remained intact. This makes sense in that the unity in the Holy Spirit is valued far more than majority rule. In this model, leadership is shared among co-equal "senior" pastors (even though we don't use the term "senior"). It seems to be good for the pastors and good for the church. We take pride, for instance, in the fact that "it was by consensus that the Quakers in the early years of the United States became the first religious community to reject the practice of slavery."

THE BEGINNING OF THE END

Is this the beginning of the end of an era? Are we hearing the death gurgles of the modern, gas-guzzling, explosive, seeker-sensitive church growth strategies? Many of us think so (or at least hope so). I'm sure that many such churches will continue to exist (technically), though many of them will continue on as a shadow of their former self. I resonate deeply with a recent comment by Jonathan Aigner in which he wrote a letter to the seeker-sensitive megachurch:

> *I'm sorry if I sound bitter. I'm not, really. More relieved than anything else. Saddened for the stories of abuse, gaslighting, and hero worship. Grieved by the commoditization of human hearts and souls, the theological void, and the liturgical collapse. But relieved that this sad chapter in American religious history is rattling to an end.*
>
> *See, the rest of us are tired. We're tired of having to compete with the downtown destination or suburban center house of entertainment that calls itself a church. We don't have the energy, we don't have the resources, we don't have the desire, but we've felt like we've had to conform - because you were growing, and we were shrinking! We felt like we had to do something drastic.*
>
> *Paranoia struck so deep in our hearts and souls that, in desperation, we cried out for your bag of tricks. So, we signed up for your silly, overpriced conferences. We copied the happy, clappy dreck you dared to call worship.*

> *We tried to find a charismatic leader like yours. We tried to be a mini-willow in our own neck of the woods. We gave up ourselves: our message, our mission, our liturgy, our identity.*
>
> *No more. We're tired. We're disillusioned. We're embarrassed. We're just done.*

Aigner goes on to call the church back to its high and holy calling: to be itself. He reminds each congregation that it is enough to simply be the family that God has created them to be, nothing more, nothing less. He pleads with us all to cease from all neurotic counting of people and all panic over empty pews. He implores us to free ourselves from our slavery to numbers. Finally, he urges us to get on with our high and holy calling:

> *So, church, it's time to rediscover your sacred, holy identity. It was never just about filling pews. Go on about the gospel that still calls to you. Go on with your liturgy. Preach the Word, administer the sacraments. Act justly, love mercy, walk humbly with God, even as it becomes more novel, more strange, and more isolating. Spread the great and glorious news!*

Amen and amen and amen. We have ceded far too much ground to the cult of speed and size and power. We have worshipped far too long at the altar of bigger, better, faster, cooler, and hipper. We have lusted far too much for the more visible, more powerful, more influential, and more popular. We have bowed down way too often to the *idol* of the *now*. As I see it, it comes down to two different ways of doing church. There are two roads a church can take. There's the way which is slow and patient and inefficient and unpopular and local and organic and most definitely does *not* "work" (by the standards of pop culture). And, there's the other way which is fast and impatient but is always efficient, always focused on "excellence," always popular, always uber-professional, and most definitely always "works" (by the standards of pop culture). If you want to build a "great" church as fast as possible, I'd recommend the *fast way*. But if you want to build a "good" church, to be yourself – your divinely created self – your Holy Spirit led self – then I'd suggest that you take the *slow and patient way*. Choose the slow meandering road. Choose the counter-cultural peculiar way of Jesus. And as you choose the slow and patient road, remember who you are. Remember how the Apostle Paul described the very messed up and very ordinary congregation at Corinth:

***"You are the Body of Christ and each one of you is a part of it."* (I Cor. 12:27)**

CHAPTER NINE

Sandbars and Backpacks

"I never bet against the mercy of God. I don't like my odds."

– Clifford Earl Brooks

One of the problems with ordinary churches is that they have ordinary pastors. Worse yet, these ordinary pastors are, of course, ordinary human beings. That means that pastors enter adulthood (and ministry) with the usual amount of issues, hang ups, blind spots, and weaknesses. Usually, after a few years, the unique pressures of ministry have, if anything, exacerbated these issues. The expectation that the pastor has his or her act together usually adds a whole new level of temptations to hide one's character defects and to present oneself as spiritually and relationally healthy which, of course, only makes things worse. In other words, even if a person is fairly well adjusted and emotionally healthy when they enter ministry, they still enter with a boatload of issues - and with a unique vulnerability towards denial and deception.

If you have any doubts that pastors go into the ministry with at least a normal amount of "baggage," find an experienced counselor or spiritual director and ask them. They will let you know that it's true: pastors are as human as anyone else, just more so. To put it another way, all of us travel through life with a backpack full of our own particular version of pain, struggle, and sin. This raises a series of questions: How messed up can a pastor be and still continue in active vocational ministry? How and where can he or she work out their issues? Should each of them have a spiritual director (counselor, mentor, sponsor) with whom they can be completely open and honest? Can a pastor be an ordinary person with ordinary friends? Can some of these close friends be members of the pastor's congregation? Allow me to discuss these questions by telling you about one of my favorite places on earth.

THE STANBAR

Before we called it the "Stanbar," we called it the "sandbar." Not just any sandbar. It was *THE* sandbar. More than that, it was OUR sandbar. I'm still not sure what a sandbar is. What I do know is that for as long as I can remember, my dad called it **the sandbar**. The other thing I know, without any doubt, even in my old age, is that it remains my favorite place on earth. As soon as I was old enough to survive the trip down there, my dad began taking me down to this sacred spot. I say "down" because it's at the bottom of one of the deepest, wildest canyons on the planet. At least, that's what my dad said. And once you go down there, you believe him. Since it's a family secret, I guess I'll have to pull a "John Gierach" on you (fly fishermen will understand) and just say that our sandbar is somewhere in the western United States. If I told you where it was, you'd never believe me anyway. In fact, until you've been there, you can't imagine how a place so wild, so rugged, so untamed, and so hard to reach, could be this close to civilization. Once you've been there, however, it immediately makes sense why we've never seen another person camp down there (outside of our family and friends). Ever.

For one, this sandbar is only reachable for a few weeks out of the year late in the fall (you'll have to trust me on that one). Second, you'd have to be fairly stupid to even try to get down there – even during the few accessible weeks between the massive Spring runoff that lasts all summer and the heavy snows which close the road in the late fall. The main reason that keeps most reasonable people away are the several (required) river crossings. Imagine, for a minute, crossing a strong, dangerous river with freezing water up to your hips. Now imagine doing this carrying a heavy backpack and walking on what seem to be bowling balls covered with "greased owl poop," as we like to put it. Now imagine doing these six times each way! Finally, if we're running late, we do this in the dark without a flash light. I told you: we're not the brightest guys on the block.

Needless to say, as I already mentioned, we pretty much have the place to ourselves. Well, more than pretty much. Completely and always, actually. My grandfather came down here as a young man. My dad came down here as a teenager. He began to take us down when we were kids. Eventually, I began to take my kids down there. Pretty soon, I'll want to take my grandkids down there. For four generations, in the late fall, we've returned to this one spot where, every spring, the raging torrents deposit fresh clean sand and an abundant supply of firewood. My lifelong friend, Clifford (who's now on his forty-second consecutive year on the sand bar), always exclaims, "Isn't God good, Joe!? Every year he piles up firewood for us and puts it right next to our camp!" So even though I've already said it, allow me to say it again: we have never, and I mean *never*, seen another human being, outside of our friends and family, camping down there (that far down the river), in over eighty years!

To make things worse, the place is sometimes too hot and other times freezing cold. It's almost always annoyingly windy. It's crawling with rattlesnakes, tarantulas, and scorpions. The canyon walls are covered in poison oak, thorny bushes, spider webs, and sheer rock walls. There are plenty of bears and mountain lions around to keep us close to the fire. No radio or cell phone reception whatsoever. We are completely lost from civilization. And we couldn't love it more. So, you ask, "what do we do?" We fish a lot and we eat a lot. But the highlight is the nightly bonfire. It's there where we tell and retell the same stories year after year, decade after decade, generation after generation. The boys listen to their dads and granddads retelling the stories, memorizing them in order to pass them on to their children. For most of our lives, my dad was the center of the sandbar. Stanley Cecil Beach was the heart and soul of this holy place. I can still picture him sitting there holding court each night, sitting on the log with his skinny legs pointed towards the fire, crossed at the ankles, his arms waving about as he talked, his broken finger pointing off in the wrong direction as he'd point at the canyon walls (an old basketball injury gone bad). He'd begin each night by telling us about each fish he'd caught that day – how he caught them and how big they were (we always knew to take off a few inches). Our favorites were the monsters "that got away." He'd describe what at first looked like a log, "as big as your leg," coming up from the bottom of the hole. He'd slap his hands together, showing how this dark torpedo slammed into his fly like a "runaway beer truck." "You don't think they're down there?" he'd ask. "Oh, there down there alright, big gnarly old German Browns, teeth like a shark." He even had names for these types of fish: "codrasters" and "snollygosters," names like that. Before long, he'd switch from fishing stories to solving the world's problems (which were all caused by the "liberals and the communists and the worthless criminals" "that should be taken out into the middle of the Atlantic Ocean and…" well, you get the point). Let's just say that we weren't raised by a non-violent Mennonite. Love, acceptance, and forgiveness were not big concepts during this stage of the evening.

Finally, though, he'd slow down, soften up a bit, and begin talking about life and death and the meaning of it all. He'd point up to the rim of the canyon several thousand feet straight up (in fact, on the north side of the canyon, it rises nearly eight thousand feet above our heads – around five thousand feet deeper than the Grand Canyon, if you can imagine). As he pointed up to the rim, he'd say, "that's the only way out of here, boys. And that's why nobody comes down here." Naturally, that always made us feel super special. A little stupid, too, but mostly special. And grateful. We'd lean back against a log and watch the hot fire's embers dance up into the night, our bellies full of wild trout, our mouths usually holding a cigar or a pipe (these were always important signs that we were grown up and that there were no women around to tell us what to do), amazed at how lucky we were to be in the company of Stanley Cecil Beach and amazed at how beautiful a billion stars are when nothing's hindering their sparkle. My dad would usually conclude the night with some statement like, "when I die, just bring my ashes down here. I mean it. Bring 'em right here. Throw me in the river and feed the fish. Or just put me in this fire."

About now, you probably want to tell me how sexist this all sounds! I know, I know. And I agree with you. My daughter reminded me often of how she was being discriminated against and how she was way overdue for her trip. I agreed with her but I told her that I couldn't convince her mom that I'd get her across the river safely. Eventually, though, she won her argument and joined us on the Stanbar. She fit right in. She was "bred for it." In addition to my dad and my children, Clifford, my brother Brian, and my two brothers-in-law, Kris and Mike, we'd sometimes bring along a close friend. Eventually, I even dragged along a few men from my church. My wife always thought that this was way too risky. Seeing their pastor sit there in his "natural habitat" telling stories, smoking a cigar, and maybe even, God forbid, taking a sip of something fermented or distilled, was just way too risky in her mind. Later, after I retired from a long career in drinking, I better understood her fears and concerns. More on that in a moment. At the time, she just thought that this would destroy any remaining respect that they had for me as their pastor! In hindsight, she probably had a point. At the time, though, I told her to relax. "What little respect they ever had for me, I'd long since destroyed," I'd reply.

You see, my wife was raised by an old school pastor. Don't get me wrong - in my opinion, he was (and still is) the best pastor in the world. But he came from a world where pastors were careful. And being careful meant that you didn't have close friends. In the old days, pastors were taught to have no close personal friends within the church. That counsel was passed on to us. We were told to keep a healthy distance from the "laity" and to maintain and project a certain pastoral image to the congregation. I was often told, "regular church people don't want their pastor to be too human." Well, as you can imagine, as soon as I heard this piece of advice, I knew that I was in big trouble! I had always been too human! I realize how poor that statement is, theologically, but you know what I mean. To make things worse, I'm so relationship-oriented and addicted to people pleasing, I make most Labrador Retrievers look like introverted cats. I often describe myself as a yellow lab on steroids. Naturally, therefore, I ignored all of the older pastor's advice and just dove right in. From the beginning, I acted like a regular person with regular friends – some super close, some not so close. After nearly forty years in one church, I still can't say if I was right or wrong. I do know, with the way I was wired, that I probably didn't have much choice in the matter. I wouldn't have survived more than a year or so without my close friends. On the other hand, I wished I'd learned – much sooner than I did – about proper boundaries and about the destructiveness of people-pleasing. In other words, I can honestly say that my close friendships saved my life on many occasions. But there were quite a few other times when they nearly destroyed my life and ministry.

I was in my late forties when I began, for the first time

in my life, to grasp concepts such as "boundaries" and "differentiation." I learned from my counselor/friend, Jerry, and from reading books, that I was the least "differentiated person" on planet earth. In other words, according to him, I had zero ability to "differentiate" between my issues and someone else's. I didn't know where mine ended and theirs began. I assumed that if someone in the world was unhappy, it was my fault and it was my job to fix it. I also assumed that everyone else would treat me the same way and not act unhappy around me. I was a total mess when it came to boundaries! I realize that this is going to shock you, but I'd been a pastor for over twenty years and I was still messed up! Can you imagine? Anyway, at one point, I was running around the church like a "one arm paper hanger in a wind storm" (as my old ski racing buddy used to put it) trying desperately to keep my best friends happy. I felt like a circus performer running on empty. I didn't have the words for it at the time, but everything within me wanted to tell them, "I just don't think I can pull that rabbit out of the hat one more week!" I wanted to say to everyone in my life: "Listen, I desperately want to be a good friend and a good pastor and a good husband and a good father and a good coach and a good son and a good brother and a good school board member and a good athletic director – but I just can't keep you all happy at the same time." I didn't realize that that wasn't my job.

In the end, though, I'm both glad and sad that I had close

friends and that I took them down to the sandbar. I'm sad because I now realize that all people, especially pastors, need to still care about things like honor and modesty and trust. I wished that I'd remembered that there is never a time when I'm not a pastor. That's simply who and what I am. But, I'm also glad. Say what you want, but I think all pastors need some people (and some places) in their lives where they can just be themselves – for better or worse. I know I do. I desperately need a place where I'm known just as Joe. "Just Joe." A place where I'm first Joe the person before I'm Joe the pastor. Just Joe the son. Joe the brother. Joe the dad. Joe the buddy. Because, before I was ever Joe the pastor, I was just Joe. And that's how these people on the sandbar have always known me and always will. Even though, over the years, I've discovered things about me that I want to grow out of, I still struggle with that tension. In other words, I don't want some things to be "just Joe" forever. I want some things to be "used to be Joe." But, still, all pastors need a sandbar in their life. Some of us need it more than breathing.

WARNING: POSSIBLE WHINING AND SELF-PITY JUST AHEAD. You don't really notice it most of the time, but it all begins to add up: the constant expectation to be super good at everything: administration, preaching, counseling, marriage, parenting, living. A disappointed look here, a criticism there, a misunderstanding, an untrue rumor, an unfavorable comparison to the pastor down the street or on the TV, and it begins to take its toll. We try to pretend that it's no big deal, but as Rob Bell puts it, "we slowly die the death of a thousand paper cuts." They add up. Don't get me wrong. As I've said, I know that we are followers of Christ. I also know what an honor and privilege it is to be called to help shepherd a flock of fellow Christ- followers. I do cherish the opportunity and embrace the responsibility. In other words, I understand that ours is a high calling. I'm just saying that it adds up. It begins to wear on us. I'm saying that Christ didn't first save us to make us religious professionals. He saved us to make us fully human. He first created us to be little boys on a river with our dads. He created us to live. To love. To play and laugh with our best friends. To eat fish and sit around a fire with our father and our children and tell stories.

On March 10th, 2005, my dad died of a cancerous brain tumor. In late September of that year, we took him at his word and carried his ashes down to the old sandbar. As usual, the fishing was good, the food was wonderful, and the campfire was great. But it wasn't the same. Without my dad, Stan Beach, Stan the Man, there was a sadness, a mild malaise, a sort of emptiness about the place. It was fitting that it rained all week. You see, my dad was more than just one of us on the sand bar. He *was* the sand bar. So much so that we renamed it the Stanbar. There is a rock wall behind our camp on the sandbar where I had decided to chisel his name into the granite. Don't worry, we know that you're not normally supposed to do that kind of thing. This was a rare exception to the rule, *take only pictures, leave only footprints*. I know all about that rule – I'm the son of a National Park Ranger! But this was different. Since we'd never seen another human being here in eighty years, we figured that it would be alright. So, one afternoon when nobody was around, I took a chisel and went over to the wall. It was lightly raining when I began. I was using a large rock for my hammer and it was slow going – much more difficult than I'd expected. Another thing I didn't expect was what began to happen to me. I guess I hadn't fully grieved the loss of my dad, my best friend. I must have done what I'd always done with painful stuff: stuffed them deep down with all the other painful stuff. Surprisingly, they began to rise up slowly from some deep place, not unlike one of those monster fish in my dad's stories. Each time I'd slam the rock into the chisel, each time a little more of my dad's name began to appear in the rock wall, I would let out a sob. For over an hour, the painful feelings of anger and loss kept emerging from my gut and erupting with deep sobs. It felt like a case of dry heaves – but what I was heaving was sorrow upon sorrow. Finally, I reached a point where I couldn't lift the rock one more time. I hadn't realized that my brother-in-law Kris had come up silently behind me. He stepped up next to me, looked into my watery eyes and then, as only a best friend on the Stanbar could have, he took the rock out of my hand, and continued the work. I don't doubt that he had a few sorrows to pour into that rock himself. Now, I realize that pastors were taught in the old days that they weren't supposed to have close friends. I don't agree. At that moment, only a close friend could have taken that rock out of my hand and know exactly what it meant.

A couple of days later, we got around to the official committal service where we'd dispose of my dad's ashes. There in front of everyone, after I, as Joe the Pastor, led us through the formalities and prayers, I, as Joe the son, broke down again and experienced another round of deep sobbing. And I didn't mind because I was in my natural habitat. I was home. I was safe on the Stanbar. I was no longer Joe the Pastor. Just Joe the son. Stan's son. The proudest son on earth. I felt like Eugene Peterson when he said, after breaking down at the pulpit during his own mother's funeral, "I've put up with all of your tears for most of my life. Now you can put up with mine."

Years ago, when I was a young man and a young pastor, I wrote a little poem about the canyon. I'm not really a poet, as you'll quickly see, but it was my rookie attempt to describe how important it was for a pastor, at least for me, to occasionally get away with close friends in a deep canyon.

CLOSE FRIENDS IN A DEEP CANYON

Wild canyon, stranger
To laughter and pain
Never

Having heard either
From wildlife or rain
Collected in head waters
High above, now roaring
Crashing boulders like pebbles
In its wake and what matters
Most is a fire shared
Embracing new dreams and
Old friends
Mainly mind-numbing rest
Belly laughter
Senseless jesting ignoring
Important complexities
Just this once…
Dearest delusion
Pretending believing that
Life is like this…
Fires and fish and malt
Distilled to take a mind
Beyond a body's terms
Warming hearts of denial
Reluctant for real mornings
Serving only
The sweet delay of inevitable
Alarm clocks
Return to joy and painful
Service…

Soul crafting
Nurturing the heart
Hardly easy or natural yet
Nothing counts as much
In the end as
The searching journey
To die happy
Knowing there's sense
In living, loving, and playing
Working, suffering, and dying.
All vanished now,
For the time being
None nagging or hindering
Struggle's over, at least
From this turn out:
Hot fires and cool nights
Close Friends in a deep canyon.

A PEEK INTO MY OWN BACKPACK

Maybe it would help to take a quick peek into my own backpack. If I could do it all over again, I'd take some time in my early twenties, before marriage and family, before seminary and ministry, and spend a year or two with a skilled therapist looking inside my backpack at my issues, blind spots, brokenness, and woundedness, etc. I'd try to get a handle on some things before jumping on the roller coaster of life, ministry, marriage, and family.

I learned, for instance, thirty years too late, that my self-identity had been greatly influenced by growing up as the smallest boy in the entire county. Throughout the all-important Junior High and Senior High years, I was so small that I was off the charts. I physically developed and matured so slowly that it greatly affected how I viewed myself and how I interacted with others. I entered High School at 4' 11' and 83 pounds. By the time I was a junior in High School and got my driver's license, I was 5' 4" (almost) and 99 pounds. Long after High School, I continued to grow and eventually reached 6 feet tall and normal weight. But it was way too late. I learned early on that if I was ever going to be accepted in society, I'd have to learn how to impress those around me with how smart, funny, and charming I was. Needless to say, these skills turned out to be both blessings and curses throughout my pastoral ministry.

I soon discovered another way to impress my friends. I learned that if I could drink more beer than anyone else and be a bit wilder than anyone else, my teammates could overlook my lack of size and strength. Even though I was a Christian, I soon developed quite a reputation and became someone Brennan Manning would have described as *an angel with an incredible capacity for beer.*

A third factor in my underdeveloped self was my parent's divorce which began during my senior year of High School. Or, to be more precise, how I failed to deal with their divorce. I will never forget receiving a letter from my older sister, Sallie, informing me that mom had kicked dad out of the house.

> **Editor's Note**: If you're wondering why the marriage ended, I can honestly say it ended over my dad's extreme obsession with sports. In our family, we played sports (especially skiing, tennis, and fishing) or watched sports or talked sports or dreamed sports – every second of every day. No exaggeration. As the story goes, my mom finally put her foot down. My mom was willing to risk the rest of her life taking a chance on romance. I can't say that I blame her – but let's just say that her next forty years were a mixed bag.

Anyway, my sister's announcement of our parent's impending divorce arrived out of the blue, without any forewarning. When I received her letter, I was riding in a truck with my friend, Steve, and I simply joked it off, threw the letter behind the seat, and laughed, "My parents are splitting up just like yours did!" I never gave it another thought – even though, decades later, with the help of a professional counselor, I learned that I probably was deeply affected by this event and that I had probably arrested my emotional development at that point – at least in the area of allowing myself to feel honest pain.

I could go on for several pages and describe for you how these negative traits and habits hurt those around me over the last forty years but suffice it to say: there's probably a better way to begin adulthood and a life of ministry than with an insecure male ego, a strong taste for beer, and the inability to feel or empathize. Years later, I finally got a handle on the ego problem, retired from drinking altogether, and even learned that I had a few feelings and opinions of my own.

The amazing thing was that I somehow survived, by the grace of God. If you think about it, it's quite simply a miracle of God's grace and patience: I've been in the same church my entire adult life. I've lived in the same house with the same family for almost all of my ministry years. Somehow, mostly by blind luck, raised four wonderful human beings. Two of my sons married and in both cases I hit the daughter-in-law jackpot. A few years later, I was just as lucky when my daughter married a fine young man. I have eight precious grandchildren (and counting). All fifteen of these "children" of mine are among my best friends, they live nearby, they love each other, love the Lord, love our church, and love hanging out at our house every Sunday afternoon. I've been a full-time pastor all these decades – I love my Amazing Grace Church family with all my heart and (somehow) they genuinely love me back. My church takes great care of me and has been nothing but gracious, generous, and patient with me over the decades. On a side note, I enjoyed twenty years as a coach on the side – at nearby local high schools -twelve years as a head tennis coach, seven years as a head baseball coach.

Believe me when I tell you that it was not easy keeping all of these balls in the air in light of all my problems, weaknesses, vulnerabilities, and bad habits. My friend, Mark, pointed out to me once that to pull all that off, I had to be one "sneaky scoundrel" (well, he actually used another word but this book is rated PG). I thought Mark's label was a bit harsh, but I knew what he meant. He was a retired airline pilot and he shared some of the same characteristics as I did. He and I both agreed that a plane full of passengers and a congregation full of parishioners share a similar assumption: both groups of people assume that their pilot/pastor is sober, knows where they're going, and knows how to get there safely. I am happy to report that he and I were both responsible and got our passengers safely to their destination. But, at the same time, he assured me that I was just like him and just as sneaky. I remember one time, I told him, "hey! God has a special place in his heart for sneaky scoundrels like us! I told him there's a famous character in the Bible named Jacob and that Jacob means "sneaky scoundrel" in Hebrew! (In actuality, the name Jacob may not contain within it the concept of deceit – but for the purposes of this story, let's go with it). He and I had a good laugh until I said, "no, really. Something like that. I'm not that far off."

I explained that Jacob came out of the womb hanging on to his twin brother's heel. He was grabbing at Esau's heel so they named him Jacob, which means something like "little heel grabber" which (I like to think) was a Hebrew idiom for "cheater or schemer" (or "sneaky scoundrel"). That's right. How'd you like to have parents that name their baby "cheater" or "schemer." If you know the story, Jacob lived up to his name, of course, and cheated and schemed his way through life until God finally got ahold of him one night on the bank of the River Jabbok. Jacob wrestled with God all night long and was wounded in the process and limped around the rest of his life. But the night of wrestling was also a kind of redemption for Jacob. He finally gave up, realized his cheatin' and schemin' days were over. He surrendered to God and God gave him a new name, "Israel," which means that God will do his fighting for him from now on. Jacob will just have to trust God to work things out instead of always taking matters into his own hand. Jacob, now called Israel, began his life in recovery from his cheating and scheming addiction. He joined a 12-step group called Cheaters Anonymous, made amends with his brother Esau, and lived the rest of his life in peaceful serenity.

Years ago, I preached a sermon on the life of Jacob, culminating with Jacob's wrestling with God on the bank of the River Jabbok (one of my favorite passages). I went home after church and that afternoon, my daughter-in-law, Brittany, said to me, "Hey Joe: I loved your sermon. You were sort of telling us your life story, weren't you?" I hadn't realized what I was doing but, in many ways, I think she was right. I think that in my later years I, too, have had to surrender to God in many areas and that I have been both wounded and healed in the process. As I limp along in the amazing grace of God, I am full of gratitude and live (usually) in a state of peaceful surrender. I still have many more lessons to learn and a few more nights wrestling with God by the River Jabbok, but I'm slowly getting the hang of this thing called life. Sort of.

My point in this chapter is this: your pastor is as human as the next person, maybe more so. Please be patient with him or her. I'm not at all saying that the "qualifications of an elder/overseer" listed in Paul's letters to Timothy and Titus are not to be taken seriously. I do think these traits, for the most part, in general, ought to be "growing realities" in a servant leader's life. I do not think, however, that these lists are exhaustive. Nor do I think that they are to be taken "hyper-literally." I like to say: if taken hyper-literally, neither Jesus nor Paul could be an elder at your church because neither is the "husband of one wife." Further, I know many servant leaders whose children did not behave well or believe fully – yet I believe these men and women were genuinely called and gifted to continue serving and leading. I know of other servant leaders who struggled in one or more areas mentioned in the lists – but continued to struggle – sometimes gaining victory – and were not disqualified for service. In my case, for instance, I'm glad to say that many of my hardest struggles are hopefully behind me and I can honestly say, by God's grace, that the old Joe doesn't live here anymore. As one of my heroes, Robbie Robertson, puts it:

Inside of the belly of the whale
Outside they was beatin' on a door
Somebody goin' down tonight
I said boys… he don't live here no more

CHAPTER TEN

The Ordinary Pastor of an Ordinary Church

"We have trouble finding the church, not because it is invisible, but because, sinful as we are, we do not particularly like what we see."

– Eugene Peterson

This chapter is for everyone, not just pastors. You may have wondered what a pastor is "good for." You may want to know how to find a good pastor. Well, I'm going to give you my best shot at answering those questions. My first point is the one I made in the previous chapter: your pastor is human. She or he is first and foremost a human being, a person trying to make their way through life just like you are. Secondly, your pastor is also a fellow regular Christian trying to follow Christ just like you are, struggling against besetting sins and temptations just like you are. If you're really lucky, your pastor is there to serve you and to be your shepherd – plain and simple – and not to further their professional career or to use you to build a bigger church or to use you as a stepping stone to another (better) church. Hopefully, your pastors are your pastors because God has appointed them to be your pastors (Acts 20:28). Hopefully, in return, God has appointed you to them (as Peter puts it, "those entrusted to you" I Peter 5:2-3). I return to Sarah Bessey's beautiful words about why she goes to church:

> *So why do I go to church? Because… we know and love our pastors for their humanity, not in spite of it. Because of the way they show up for us. Because sometimes it's an amazing sermon and sometimes it's, um, not.*

I was very lucky to have heard a sermon from Eugene Peterson, in person, which is still my all-time favorite sermon. It was called "What's a Pastor Good For?" It was directed at pastors but I think that in this one respect it applies to all of us. Let's begin with his beautiful description of the church and the pastor's calling:

> *I realized that this was my place and work in the church, to be a witness to the truth that dazzles gradually. I would be a witness to the Holy Spirit's formation of congregation out of this mixed bag of humanity that is my congregation – broken, hobbled, crippled, sexually abused and spiritually abused, emotionally unstable, passive and passive-aggressive, neurotic men and women. Men at fifty who failed a dozen times and know that they*

will never amount to anything. Women who have been ignored and scorned and abused in a marriage in which they have been faithful. People living with children and spouses in addictions. Lepers and blind and deaf and dumb sinners. Also, fresh converts, excited to be in on this new life. Spirited young people, energetic and eager to be guided into a life of love and compassion, mission, and evangelism. A few seasoned saints who know how to pray and listen and endure. And a considerable number of people who pretty much just show up. I wonder why they bother. There they are. The hot, the cold, and the lukewarm, Christians, half-Christians, almost Christians. New-agers, angry ex-Catholics, sweet new converts. I didn't choose them. I don't get to choose them.

And this is what Pastors are good for: we're good for taking a long, loving look at these people. It doesn't seem at all obvious at first, but when we keep at it, persist in this long, loving look, we realize that we are, in fact, looking at the church, this Holy Spirit-created community that forms Christ in this place.

I would add that this is what any Christian is good for. Peterson goes on to say that if we don't develop this long, loving look, we'll get this romantic illusion of what a church could be or should be, and then something terrible happens:

THE CHURCH WE WANT BECOMES THE ENEMY OF THE CHURCH WE HAVE.

No, for better or worse, we need to recognize that this ordinary congregation to which we belong is indeed Corpus Christi, the body of Christ, the form that our Lord has chosen to take in the world. Peterson writes that "we have trouble finding the church, not because it is invisible, but because, sinful as we are, we do not particularly like what we see."

Please forgive me for including another long quote but I must. This one is from Lewis Smedes and is one of my all-time favorites on the subject of *what a pastor is good for*. I've often had to remind myself to re-heed his message:

> *I made more than my share of mistakes [during my first pastorate] - But there was one mistake I made early on that was all but unforgiveable. I forgot that the worshippers whom I was called to serve were ordinary people – not leaders, not educated, not wealthy, just working people – and would never be anything else. I wanted them to be leaders, visionaries... and in my heart I faulted them for not fitting my notion of what I wanted them to be. Then I remembered what my former professor of church history told me the night that I was ordained. Walking into the church with him, I asked him if he had one last piece of advice for me. "Yeah," he said, "just*

> *remember that the people of your church are ordinary people. If you take them as they are, you will do OK." I did sometimes forget that I was called to serve these people, not the elite Christians that I wished they were. When I did forget, I was ineffective, unloving, impatient, wretched. As time went by, however, and as I learned more about myself, I knew that I was just as weak, just as limited, just as insecure, just as boring, just as frightened – and just as sinful – as they were. When I finally got that fact firmly lodged in my soul, I became, I think, a passable servant.*

I mentioned earlier how Eugene Peterson, on many occasions, said that every time he moves to a new community, he finds a church nearby and just becomes a part of it. Every time someone asks him how to find a good church, he advises them to do what he does: find a church nearby. Every time he finds a church, he finds a bunch of regular people. Then he says, in one of his all-time classic passages:

> *Every once in a while, a shaft of blazing beauty seems to break out of nowhere and illuminate these companies, and then I see what my sin-dulled eyes had missed: word of God-shaped, Holy Spirit-created lives of sacrificial humility, incredible courage, heroic virtue, holy praise, joyful suffering, constant prayer, persevering obedience. I see Christ...*

...For Christ plays in ten thousand places,
Lovely in limbs, and lovely in eyes not his
To the Father through the features of men's faces.
(Peterson quoting Gerald Manley Hopkins)

Rich Mullins tells a story about some young Christians who left his church in Wichita and went over to the church with the "best worship in town" (which at the time was a Vineyard church). They said they were looking for "anointed worship," worship that gave them "Holy Spirit goosebumps." When they got there, they were met by a very wise pastor. When the pastor heard why they had come, he instructed them to go back to their home church. He explained to them that in a few years this worship here would also become familiar, they would become bored again, and they'd be off again in search of better worship and better goosebumps – better worship *somewhere else*, of course, always *somewhere else*. Then he explained to them that they would continue to do this their entire lives and would end up not helping any church. And, he said, they would likely never grow up. They would probably remain immature children looking for excitement in all the wrong places. He told them that they would likely spend their lives unimpressed by their own ordinary church family – choosing instead to fantasize about how wonderful it would be to be *somewhere else*. When people view their spouses or children in this same way, we are scandalized. But millions of men and women view their church family in exactly this way: "raving" about every exciting church they visit and every church they see online or in magazines.

LEADERSHIP IS OVERRATED

I believe that a local church ministry should avoid, at all costs, the temptation to expect its pastors to function as CEO's, business managers, entrepreneurs, etc. Even the term "leadership" is an easily abused and misused concept and, I believe, almost always harmful to the church and to the gospel when it is viewed through the interpretive lens of modern American culture. Even when (mis)using Old Testament leadership models, we must be extremely cautious. I believe that mis-using and mis-applying Old Testament leadership models can be just as damaging as mis-using and mis-applying the Old Testament models of warfare, slavery, or polygamy. The New Testament model of pastoral leadership is that of a team of pastors – the plurality of elders. The marks of these servant-leaders are humility, love, mutual submission, mutual respect, consensus, deference to one another, putting others first, and saturation in the Word, prayer, doctrine, and relationships. I see no place whatsoever for a "strong" and "decisive" single leader – a New Testament version of Moses, leading the people of God through the wilderness. Rather, I see a team of "brothers" and "sisters," a team of servant-leaders. We should "lead" with the words of Jesus ringing in our ears: "it is not so among you."

Now, I fully realize that pastors are required by common sense and the scriptures to do some management. I understand that the Bible does make a reference to the elders managing the local church. My undergraduate degree is in Business Management. I understand that, to some degree, the church is a "corporation" with certain business-like concerns and that those concerns must be run somewhat "business-like." But I strongly believe that pastors and congregations should view this as a necessary evil and not as the pastor's primary identity. I'm not saying that being well organized is wrong (although I'm tempted). I'm just saying that the business side of our calling should be kept to a minimum.

I'm probably overstating things a bit… but allow me to put it this way: pastors should never exchange their call to pray, study, preach, teach, and care for souls, for the world's pottage. Pastors are not to have an office; they are to have a study. They are to primarily deal with prayer, the word, and the spiritual direction of people; *not* with telephones, agendas, and strategies. They are to think more biblically than organizationally. They are to focus more on God and people than they are on programs, buildings, and plans. They are to keep in step with the Spirit, not with the latest marketing and technological gimmicks. Maybe the best way to put it is to say that our leadership style should approximate that of Jesus Christ's. Philip Yancey captured the key elements like this:

> *Sometimes I wonder how Jesus would have fared in this day of mass media and high-tech ministry. I can't picture him worrying about the details of running a large organization. I can't see him letting some make-up artist improve his looks before a TV appearance. And I have a hard time imagining the fundraising letters Jesus might write.*

Jesus was, by today's standards, inefficient and lacking professional ambition. He didn't even "get busy" in the ministry until he was thirty years old. At that time, he only spent three years at it. Most of the time, he maintained a very leisurely pace. He focused the vast majority of his time on twelve ragamuffins, one of which was a crook. He spent a lot of his time praying, walking, telling stories, and attending dinner parties at people's houses. He is portrayed numerous times as hanging out with friends (many of whom had questionable characters), but we are told of very few times when Jesus ever did anything that was even remotely "business-like." Rather than showing any ambition to gain and maintain a large following, he did everything he could to keep the crowd small and simple. Jesus told people to keep his miracles secret. When crowds did try to follow him, he often fled to solitude, or rowed across a lake. One time, when they wanted to make him their king, his getaway was even quicker than usual. He was never once guilty of false advertising. We're told that Jesus would turn around to the crowd and make it crystal clear, right up front, that following him wasn't easy or user-friendly. It wasn't convenient. It wasn't big on family values. He said things like, "you cannot be my disciple unless…"

It just seems patently obvious to me that there is a stark contrast between the leadership style of Jesus and the one pushed on us these days. I find it odd that I have never heard a church-growth expert even raise this question, let alone answer it: if our Lord, Master, and Savior had the reputation of being a glutton, a wino, a friend of sinners, unprofessional, and consistently anti-crowd, anti-sensational, and anti-marketing, then what in the world is wrong with us? These are the last things that we'd ever be accused of. Now, as we all know, Jesus never sinned. But I think we all also know exactly what I mean by my question, and I'm still waiting for a good answer.

THE ANTI-VISION: *Bonhoeffer in Plain Language*

To those unfortunate co-pastors of mine over the years, it probably looked like I was opposed to the idea of "excellence" in the church's programs, presentation, marketing, church growth, organizational efficiency, corporate vision, etc. To a large extent, they would be correct in that perception. I've been accused of this more than once. I usually comfort myself with thoughts like, "well, so was Jesus." But, of course, I later remember that Jesus probably doesn't share all of my opinions and preferences. So, I admit it. It is an actual weakness of mine: anti-program to a fault. But, I also do think we tend to over-emphasize organizational efficiency and professional polish over people and relationships. As I just mentioned, I am not very interested in anything usually related to "leadership." I am not anti-growth, per se. I am just opposed to most of the principles, values, and approaches of the church growth movement.

Finally, I am also anti-vision if the "vision" contains even a hint of a personal ego-driven vision. It's very difficult, if not impossible, to separate our "vision" for a church from our "vision" of a successful ministry career. Sadly, as far as I can tell, the latter usually trumps the former. This was never more obvious than when a famous pastor who bragged in his books that he would fire his staff members (even if they had been lifelong close friends and colleagues) as soon as he determined that their talent levels had "taken him as far as they could." He would fire them because they "weren't cut out to take him to the next level." Many pastors I know share my dislike of the word "vision" when used in this way. These same pastors also share my distaste for spending year after year after year trying to come up with a "vision statement" for our church. Almost always, by the time we arrive at such a definitive statement - the church and its context has changed so much it's time to start over.

Years ago, the late great Internet Monk, Michael Spencer, reminded us that Abraham Lincoln was often accused of lacking vision. At the same time, Lincoln was accused of having no moral standard. He was accused of being a poor leader. His motto became "My policy is to have no policy" – a motto that infuriated the sober, doctrinaire people around him who thought that the president lacked principles as well. My point is this: I am against vision if by vision one means personal professional ambition. I am anti-vision if it means corporate long-term goals. I am fully aware of the proverb, "Without a vision, the people perish." But I'm also aware that vision in that context means "revelation." Yes, without a word from God, the people perish. I fully agree. It is truth we need, not another corporate business plan for rapid growth. What's a pastor good for? A pastor is good for bringing a "word from elsewhere" and not for bringing another exciting five-year expansion plan. That phrase comes from Walter Brueggemann. I've attached it to our pulpit: "Bring a word from elsewhere or get out of the pulpit." We need a word from Isaiah and Ezekiel more than we need a word from Apple or Google.

You can imagine my joy upon discovering Dietrich Bonhoeffer's proclamation: "God hates visionary dreaming." Bonhoeffer explains the reason why: because visionary dreaming hates and destroys the community that already exists as it is. After fifteen or twenty years of full-time pastoral ministry, I had already grown sick and tired of all the self-appointed prophets and visionaries that come into a pastor's life, suggesting new and better ways to grow a church – and by "grow" they always mean "bigger, better, faster." During those days, I often returned to a book I'd discovered in my days in seminary: the book by Dr. Dietrich Bonhoeffer, his 1938 work, *Gemeinsames Leben.* This seminal work was translated into English in 1954 and entitled, *Life Together*. Bonhoeffer's insightful diagnosis of our community-destroying disease is found in the section entitled, "Christian Community is not a human ideal but rather a divine reality." The following are some nearly word-for-word excerpts (with a few editorial liberties taken along the way – think of this as "The Message" version of Bonhoeffer).

> *He who loves his own vision or agenda more than the actual Christian community that God has called him to, becomes a destroyer of that community... In this sense,* ***God hates visionary dreaming****; it makes the dreamer proud and pretentious. The man who fashions a visionary ideal of a community demands that it be realized by God, by others, and by himself... When things do not go the dreamer's way, he calls the effort a failure. So, the dreamer is left with no other option. He must become, first an accuser of his brethren, then an accuser of God, and finally the despairing accuser of himself.*

I had even more fun paraphrasing a section from Bonhoeffer

that reminded me of the wisdom of Lewis Smedes referred to above. What is a pastor good for? A pastor is good for standing with his or her congregation, for advocating for the congregation, for waiting for her, for serving her, for pleading to God for her. Here's Bonhoeffer paraphrased again:

> *A pastor should not complain about his congregation, certainly never to other people, but also not even to God… A congregation has not been entrusted to him in order that he should become its accuser before God and men. Satan is already doing a fine job in the area of complaint and accusation. When a person becomes alienated from a Christian community in which he has been placed and begins to raise complaints about it, he had better examine himself first to see whether the trouble is not due to his flawed and naïve "vision" of what a church can and should be. Let him consider the probability that God wants to shatter his visionary dream and, thus, making him a humble, useful servant… Let him, aware of his own guilt, make intercession for these precious sheep God has called him to love. Let him do what he is committed and ordained to do, and to thank God for the immeasurable privilege of that calling… When the morning mists of dreams vanish and personal agendas evaporate… then dawns the bright day of Christian fellowship.*

The Apostle Paul put it this way: "*...we were not just pretending to be your friends... but we were as gentle among you as a mother feeding and caring for her own children. We loved you so much that we gave you not only God's Good News but our own lives, too.*" (I Thess. 2:5, 7-8; NLT). The Apostle Peter put it this way: "*Care for the flock of God entrusted to you. Watch over it willingly, not grudgingly... Don't lord it over the people assigned to your care...*" (2 Peter 5:2-3; NLT)

Christian fellowship is not an *ideal* to be realized through hard work and proper management; it is rather a *reality* created by God in Christ in which we may participate if we are willing to receive it with humility and gratitude. The more clearly and quickly we realize that our fellowship together in a Christian congregation… is sheer gift and is built in and through Jesus Christ alone, the more joyfully we will minister to our flock – the more we will love it, pray for it, believe in it, encourage it, be its main cheerleader and defender, and hope the best for it. And then, and only then, will the congregation follow our lead onward and upward to higher ground. To quote a wise man, "once you've won a congregation over with your love, acceptance, and pure motives… they'd storm the gates of hell with squirt guns if you asked them to."

About nine years ago, I was sitting in my office reflecting on the previous week. I had just spent the week with Eugene and Jan Peterson up in Estes Park, Colorado. Only hours before, I received the most gracious thank you letter from Eugene and I was overflowing with gratitude. What a blessing to have spent quality time with my mentor! Anyway, as I sat there, these words poured out of me:

We can either tremble or trust,
worry or worship,
panic or pray.
We can either take the broad way or the narrow way.
We can either push our pastors into playing the world's game
and into trying to do God's work in the devil's way,
Or we can encourage him or her to spend time
picking stones out of the brook.

Let them (better, make them) spend their time
in prayer, in God's Word, in being with their brothers and sisters,
in their study (don't let them call it an office),
in their pulpit, at their lectern,
in the community, and in the world.

Help them to be prophets, preachers, pray-ers, and poets.
Forbid them to political pushers, propagandists,
promoters, pamphleteers, or programmers.

No one could have guessed that the person

picking stones out of the brook
was doing the most significant work of the day.

At Eugene Peterson's memorial service, his son Leif Peterson, revealed that he used to joke with his father and tell him, "you only have one sermon, dad. One message." Leif would say this despite his dad writing over thirty books, despite his dad having spent decades of creativity in sharing the Bible with people in new ways. In a poem he created for the memorial service, Leif said to his dad, "It's almost laughable how you fooled them, how for thirty years every week you made them think you were saying something new. They thought you were a magician in your long black robe hiding so much in your ample sleeves, always pulling out something fresh and making them think it was just for them," he continued. "They didn't know how simple it all was. They were blind to your secret." Leif Peterson said that he knew his father's secret, however, as his dad had been sharing it with him for a lifetime. "For 50 years you steal into my room at night and whispered softly to my sleeping head. It's the same message over and over:"

God loves you. He's on your side.
He's coming after you. He's relentless.

What's a pastor good for? That's what a pastor is good for.

CHAPTER ELEVEN

Front Row Seats

"I simply continue to be amazed by how easily we leave our local church. Somewhere along the line we became the kinds of people for whom the church means very little. We're a promiscuous people."

- Sean Palmer

Being a pastor has its perks. And I'm not just talking about things like the favorable "housing allowance" in our tax laws (a holdover from the old parsonage days). Speaking of taxes: yes, pastors do have to pay taxes just the same as everyone else, except for that one benefit. No, I'm speaking more about all of the other perks and advantages. For starters, many of us get to do what we love. Many of us have very flexible schedules. We can take time off – on the spur of the moment - for special events, for visiting friends and relatives, or just to take hikes or bike rides when the weather is perfect. We get to attend exciting lectures and conferences and call them "continuing ed." Many pastors receive long vacations (and occasionally even sabbaticals) to refresh, renew, and prepare for another season of ministry.

One of my favorite perks: I was able to attend every single event in my children's life: academic events, sports, field trips, recitals, lessons, you name it. And I do mean every single event. All four of my children attended an elementary school that met in our church building. If any of them were doing anything in their classes, I just had to pop out of my office and join them. Even after they went off and attended other schools, I was able to run over and catch their events. After they all grew up, I realized how unbelievably lucky I had been to have been present for every single moment of their growing up years. There are not many vocations, not many professions, that would allow for such a blessing.

There are other perks as well. Most of us get to stand up and talk for a half an hour every week while a room full of people listen politely to our every word (or at least try to appear so). I often wonder how many times a man or woman in the congregation, during or after a sermon, has a profound thought or question burning within them – which never gets expressed. Yet a preacher gets to share every single thought that enters his or her mind – however profound or inane. We often are treated with honor and respect - usually much more than we deserve. We are usually no more sacrificial or faithful than many dedicated brothers and sisters in our church - and often less so – but we are often treated with great respect. We are given extra time to study, to read, to attend conferences, to interact with other pastors and leaders, with renowned teachers, writers, and scholars – resulting in us being revered as the local "Bible Answer Man" (or woman). Sadly (I'm guilty of this one), we often repay this privilege by wondering why everyone doesn't understand the Bible as well as we do! On top of all that, all of this extra study time comes after we were afforded, several years ago, the rare privilege of studying Scripture and theology with great teachers at a seminary.

One of the best perks, though, is having a *front row seat* to many of life's most important moments: birth, death, marriage, baptism, conversion, healing, reconciliation, and other such special and sacred moments. Pastors, of course, do far more than simply deal with birth, marriage, and death – or as they say, "hatch, match, and dispatch." I must admit, however, that few other vocations allow us to experience that sacred moment of holding an infant in one's arms and lifting them up to the Lord in a prayer of dedication or in an act of baptism. Few people have the privilege to be close enough to see the tears forming in the eyes of the bride as her groom repeats his vows or the almost imperceptible shaking of the groom's hand as he attempts to hold the ring on her finger. Few others are there to see the wide-eyed wonder on the face of the baptismal candidate as she ascends out of the baptismal waters. How many people have the awesome privilege to sit with a man as he watches his elderly dad take his last breath? Or, the honor of walking with a teenager through the valley of the shadow of death as he or she watches their mother take her last breath? At other times, few moments in life are as sacred as that moment when we look into the face of a broken, humbled, repentant sinner asking for God's mercy at the altar.

Sometimes, the pastoral ministry provides us with front row seats to moments that are at once sacred and tragic. I will never ever forget the day when our dear friends, Scott and Sarah, lost their three-year-old son, Christian, right before our very eyes. We stood at the nurse's station in the center of an intensive care unit watching a team of doctors and nurses work feverishly to keep their son alive. After what seemed like fifteen or twenty minutes of working and shouting, it suddenly stopped without warning. Instant and total silence. The head doctor turned to walk slowly toward us and, of course, didn't need to say a word. We all knew. The young father, tall and strong, slowly sank to the floor as I sank with him and we just sat together. His wife and my wife did the same. There were no words to be said at that moment. Only dark pain and emptiness. What I'm saying is that, as horrifically painful as those moments are, there is a sacred holiness to them as well. To walk with someone through the valley of the shadow of death is a holy privilege. And pastors experience this hundreds of times over the years.

So, before I mention some of the painful and stressful aspects of being a pastor, please hear me well: in many respects, many of us pastors have it made. I, for sure, am one of those pastors. Compared to many of the people in my congregation and in the neighborhood surrounding my church, I have it easy. For over thirty years, my congregation has treated me extremely well. I am well cared for in every respect. I have ended every single day of my adult life going to bed in a safe comfortable home. I have never had to worry about having enough food to eat or clothes to wear. I have always had more than enough of everything. I've enjoyed frequent vacations and countless blessings. I have nothing to complain about. The church has freed me up to pastor, preach, study, and care for people. They have generously taken care of my needs. I am eternally grateful for my loving and generous congregation. Many, if not most, of the men and women in my congregation have not had it so well. Many of them have had to work two or three jobs just to survive. Many of them have had to live with extreme financial pressure and stress. Many of them go years without a single vacation. I have nothing to complain about.

HOWEVER...

Unfortunately, however, having front row seats is also one of the worst things about being a pastor. We also get front row seats to an unusual amount of abandonment, rejection, gossip, and criticism. I believe that pastors get to experience these things in a way that is unique among all the vocations. Don't get me wrong – there are similar stresses with all positions of leadership and authority. Anytime a person is a teacher, a superintendent, a manager, a director, a coach, a president, or any other leadership position, they inevitably receive constant criticism. All complaints must flow somewhere and they inevitably flow upward to the top. That just comes with the position. I realize that, of course, there's truth to the adage: "if a leader can't stand the heat they need to get out of the kitchen."

I still believe, though, that there are some unique pressures and stresses inherent in the pastoral vocation. There's a reason that there are such high rates of depression, burnout, suicide, divorce, and moral failure among pastors. One of the main sources of pain, in my experience and in my opinion, is this: we get front row seats to watch dear friends, over and over, one by one, walking out of our life. Not many other vocations place a person in a position to receive as many ugly letters or angry phone calls full of unfair criticisms and complaints - often from close friends - and often couched in the well-known and well-meaning words: "we just think God is moving us along."

Far worse than the letters and calls, though, are the countless times that close friends walk away without a word. The young people call this phenomenon "ghosting" (when a close friend suddenly and without warning simply disappears from your life). This may be the most painful of all. Even now, as I put the finishing touches on this book during the Spring of 2019, I am currently being *ghosted* by four friends in the church. Just sudden disappearances. Vanished, apparently, for no discernable reason. No response to numerous texts, voice mails, emails, etc. It happens on a regular basis but never ceases to hurt. Every pastor I know (I can't think of a single exception) has had their hearts ripped out so many times, by so many people, that they've lost count. I know I have. And, strangely, these close friends that suddenly and mysteriously vanish are almost always the very people that we've poured our lives into the most, the people that we've come to love and trust the most. If I had a magic wand, I'd have pastors and their friends always treat each other with common decency and respect.

The temptation, of course, is to develop thick skin and keep our distance. And yet, we realize that this isn't really living. So, we risk again... only to have our hearts ripped out once again. My friend, pastor Brian Zahnd, was interviewed recently and the first question he received was: *What has been your worst moment as a pastor?* His answer:

> *I'll answer in terms of moments (plural), because they belong to a painful genre. People come and go in churches, that's just reality of church life in the consumerist context of North America. I accept that. But when long time members and friends leave, and do so*

> *with malice and ill-will, this can be extremely painful. When I began to lead Word of Life Church beyond the narrow confines of God-and-Country, Self-Help, Americanized evangelicalism, I had some close friends turn on me with a viciousness that was stunning... I'm sure most pastors know what I'm talking about.*

This doesn't mean that people *never* have a good reason to leave a fellowship of Christians. God sometimes calls people into ministries elsewhere. Sometimes, people have to move because of a change in jobs, marital status, education, and many other reasons. Sometimes, people have to move on because of divorce or other relational strains or hurtful wounds that are just too painful to endure. Once in a while, sadly, there are theological convictions or philosophical differences that simply can't be overcome. Some people are genuinely moving in a different direction than the church or the pastor is moving (theologically or otherwise) - or vice versa. Other times, the church is continuing on its pilgrimage and some people remain stuck in the "safe, familiar, and comfortable" ditch of the past ("this church just isn't the same anymore" or "I don't like where this church is going" or "who stole my church?"). Finally, we must admit: sometimes people leave because the pastor just plain messes up. No pastor is perfect and sometimes they deeply offend a brother or sister through neglect, anger, or other inappropriate behavior. All pastors, sooner or later, either intentionally or inadvertently, mishandle a person, a family, or a situation, and will lose some friends in the process. Of course, there are the extreme cases of actual criminal abuse which are tragic and horrendous beyond words. Most of the time, however, the truth remains: there a few good reasons to leave one's own church and hundreds of bad reasons.

The wife of a close friend emailed me one day. Her husband is a pastor out on the West Coast (I'll call him Richard). Her email:

> *Tonight, everyone's an idiot. I'm hacked off at a Dear John letter I got today from a church member. Twenty years, and this family is quitting church with a FACEBOOK MESSAGE?? At this point, I don't even think I'm going to reply. Joe, lately I've been thinking I'm not sure I can keep doing this pastor thing the rest of my life. Say a prayer for me. Don't say anything to Richard. I didn't tell him about it. He knows they're leaving. Everyone knows. They've talked to lots of others. Just not us. I'll be all right. Just need to blow off a little steam.*

THE SUFFERINGS OF CHRIST

The Sufferings of Christ. Those words were spoken over me one day by Pastor Ben Patterson. I was at the National Pastors'

Conference in San Diego. I had also attended the previous year's conference at which I'd had lunch with Pastor Ben. At this lunch the year before, I had shared my longstanding painful frustration with the feeling of being censored (in my teaching and preaching). For over a decade I had been battling this frustration. Every time I ran across a seasoned veteran or "sage" such as Ben Patterson, I would invariably ask them the same question. "How do you deal with this overwhelming, stifling sense of censorship in the pulpit or in small groups?" So, naturally, I did the same thing when I had the chance to be with Ben. I poured out my heart to him for an hour. I explained that I was suffocating under what felt like a heavy political correctness within my own church. I explained that even my closest friends, family members, and colleagues would often react if I said anything that went against the commonly held assumptions of the Christian sub-culture (typically anything having to do with Israel, the rapture, heaven/hell, nationalism, etc.). I assured him that I wasn't implying that I thought I was "right" or correct in all my opinions. I was talking about the crazy assumptions among my friends that had no basis in church history, theology, or the scriptures. On truly debatable subjects I have no problem with genuine disagreement.

I explained to Ben how I would often whine to my family and friends, "I can't explain what the Bible really teaches! I can't tell people the truth!" I explained that sometimes I even want to go all Colonel Jessup from the pulpit and scream, "you can't handle the truth!" I worked at convincing Pastor Ben that I wasn't just making this up and that I wasn't just being overly sensitive or cowardly. I gave him several examples of things we can't explain from the pulpit and subjects we can't touch or we'll be run out of town.

As I said, Ben Patterson listened patiently and graciously. In the end, however, I think he hit me right between the eyes with some truth I needed. He said things like, "Well, what do you expect? You've been to seminary, you've been given a mind that loves theology, you get freed up by the church to study and think and go to these fancy conferences. You should be a few steps ahead of your congregation in understanding some things and, if you're not, shame on you." He said things like, "you're lucky. You get to plant seeds in people. You have the rare privilege of having front row seats to some light bulbs coming on in people's heads after they grow out of some these enculturated assumptions. You get to witness miraculous paradigm shifts. You've got to stop viewing this as a problem and, instead, receive it as a blessed opportunity to be used by God to plant seeds." I recalled Eugene Peterson telling me the same thing. He often exhorted us pastors to have the courage to tell all the truth but to make sure to "tell it slant" (borrowing from Emily Dickenson). He'd frequently quote her words and remind us that the truth must "dazzle gradually or every man be blind."

Ben Patterson then began to dig deeper. He asked me, “how long have you been teaching and preaching at your church?” I said, “all my adult life. Over thirty years.”

Ben continued, “I think your people trust you more than you give them credit. I think you could push them quite a bit further than you think you can. Have you ever seen those trainers that have a person lay down on the ground and they’ll take the person’s leg and stretch it back over their heads?” “Yeah,” I replied.

He said, “Well, when the person knows the trainer and trusts the trainer, they’ll let the trainer stretch their leg as far over as they can. It’s like that with you and your church. They know you and trust you more than you think. You need to trust God and trust your instincts and stop whining.”

I took Ben Patterson’s words to heart. A year later, though, I ran into him out at the same place. I had some friends with me and they got to overhear his words as well. After I reacquainted myself with him, he said, “Joe, I’ve honestly prayed for you this entire year. Frequently. How’d it go?” I was a bit ashamed to admit that I still struggled mightily all year with the same frustration of feeling censored and handcuffed and silenced. He just looked at me and answered, “The sufferings of Christ.” His words have reverberated in my mind and heart for a decade since he said them (as well as in the hearts of my friends who overheard him say this). His words have helped me tremendously but I'm still ashamed to admit that I struggle to this day with the feeling of having front row seats to censorship. I still yearn for the freedom (or the courage) to speak the truth in love. I still hate that feeling that the pop culture has had much more influence on my brothers and sisters in the church than all our teaching ever could. I still grieve over my friends and loved ones in the church being thoroughly discipled by the evangelical pop culture. I'm trying to remember the wisdom I've received from the sages, but it's still tough. I still hate to see my loved ones turning into puppets. I do love being a shepherd, please believe me. But it often feels like my fellow sheep are being raised by wolves at home and being discipled by cable news and popular Christian junk food (which can be easily found in Christian books, Christian television, Christian radio, websites, and schools - both public and Christian. I can relate to the pastor in the book *Gilead*:

> *Two or three of the ladies had pronounced views on points of doctrine, particularly sin and damnation, which they never learned from me. I blame the radio for sowing a good deal of confusion where theology is concerned. And television is worse. You can spend forty years teaching people to be awake to the fact of mystery and then some fellow with no more theological sense than a jackrabbit gets himself a radio ministry and all your work is forgotten. I do wonder where it will all end.*

I've had close friends leave the church because they became obsessed with "junk food" teaching about prophecy and the book of Revelation and other kinds of garbage that you can find on the internet, radio, and television. We weren't serving up that sensational junk food, so they left. At times like that, it seems nearly impossible to be a pastor in America. My friend often tells me, "actually, Joe, it *is* impossible. Not just hard. Impossible." I know what he means. He means that to be a genuine pastor in modern secularized America is to be called, like Jeremiah, to an impossible task.

I'm reminded of something Eugene Peterson told us as we sat with him having lunch at a restaurant in Orlando, Florida: "Politics trumps everything" (this was seven years before that would become a pun). He had just told a story of how one of his most faithful parishioners at his church in Maryland had retired and moved to Texas. This man, this close friend of his, had sat under Eugene's preaching nearly every year for over twenty years. But, in his retirement, this friend had sent Eugene a letter which inadvertently revealed that Eugene had hardly affected the man's theology one iota. The letter revealed that the former parishioner had adopted nearly every misguided assumption of the American pop-culture in general, and of the evangelical pop-culture in particular. In other words, when all was said and done, the man had not been discipled by Eugene Peterson (and the gospel of Christ) but, instead, had been thoroughly and effectively discipled by the pop culture. **Politics trumps everything.**

Now, if you're reading this and you're not a pastor, you might be thinking "yes, but what about the pain that pastors inflict upon us people? What about the pain and suffering that these families are going through? What about those times when a pastor truly does mess up and is guilty of neglect or genuine offense? What about genuine disagreements over theology or genuine philosophical differences?" Those are good questions. As I said, there are indeed times when a person or family has good reason to move on. There are indeed times when the pastor is just flat out wrong or sinful or negligent. There are times of genuine disagreement. There are times when a person or a family is going through deep pain - and simply can't talk about it. I understand. I really do. And I know that pastors need to assume the best and to not assume that everything is about them. Pastors need to spend time trying to enter into that pain, help out if possible, pray, teach, and love. And, as I said before, pastors need to spend a lot of time learning how to love and forgive. If pastors don't become master forgivers, they will be destroyed in the process. Quoting Bell again, *if pastors don't become master forgivers, they will die the death of a thousand paper cuts.*

I guess what I (and most other pastors) would want is that our brothers and sisters would simply come to us "early and often" with any honest questions or concerns - *before* those questions or concerns become major problems. Believe it or not, we pastors can handle someone leaving for another church. We just feel that we've earned the right to an honest conversation before being ghosted by a good friend. Almost always, when someone has asked me early on about something they heard or thought, it turns out to be a misunderstanding. Sometimes, a person will have a perfectly sensible and practical reason why they can't attend church anymore. In these cases, pastors just like a quick explanation rather than a mysterious silence.

Anyway, that's the good, the bad, and the ugly of having front row seats to life's best and worst moments. In the end, I cherish the privilege and honor and blessing of being called to be a servant leader. My family at Amazing Grace Church has been extremely faithful, generous, and supportive. I often feel that I hit the congregation jackpot. I thank God every day for my brothers and sisters in the body of Christ. Amen.

CHAPTER 12

The Ten Theses of the Ordinary Church

"Salvation is a kind of belonging."

– Brian Zahnd

† **The church in America is suffering because a high percentage of individual American Christians are just that: *individuals.***
We are in desperate need of more lofty ecclesiology. Our low level of commitment to the local ordinary church is killing us and is harming the nation as a whole. (The other major problem with us American Christians is that we are first *Americans* and only secondarily *Christians* – but that's for another book).

† **We follow Christ - *together through life* – or we don't follow him at all.** From the very first step of faith, we follow Christ into the kingdom of God. We do it together.

Yes, we *personally* follow Christ but we do it together or we don't do it at all. From the moment we say "yes" to Christ, we say "yes" to his church. When we say "yes" to the King, we say "yes" to his Kingdom. When we say "yes" to the Father, we say "yes" to his family. We cannot have one without the other. One Christian is NO Christian.

† **Salvation is a kind of belonging.**
Becoming a Christian is a kind of *joining,* a kind of *belonging*. The moment a person says "yes" to Jesus' invitation to follow him, he or she steps into a kingdom, a body, a movement, a fellowship of disciples. I like to say something that makes people upset, so I'll say it here: "he or she might be saved, but they're not a Christian." Being a Christian isn't first a matter of where you go when you die. It's first a matter of inclusion into the covenant people of God – in this life and in the life to come. God doesn't just want us to go to heaven *after* we die - he wants us to go to heaven *before* we die. And we do that by entering into the kingdom of heaven (now).

† **The Kingdom of God, and the (universal/invisible) church of God, always and only manifests itself in actual, visible, local congregations.**
These churches (congregations) are "outposts" of the Kingdom, little advance "colonies" or "beachheads" of the heaven-on-earth which is to come. These congregations

gather regularly to worship God (praise, fellowship, prayer, proclamation and teaching, Holy Communion, baptism). Each local congregation isn't just a "part" of the overall body of Christ – the congregation *is* the body of Christ.

† **The church is the family of God. We follow Christ "together through life" as part of an actual church family.**
The church is our first family. It is a family of God at worship and a family on a mission but it remains a family. And "it" is an actual congregation. In other words, we follow Christ together with people that we know and who know us (this includes pastors we know and with pastors who know us). We do this with people unlike us - different ages, races, personalities, theological preferences, political parties, and different musical preferences. This is by design. We unite, in spite of our differences, around our highest allegiance, around our common bond in the Lord Jesus Christ.

† **The ordinary, regular, every day, garden variety local church, with all of its obvious flaws and shortcomings, is the glory of God.**
It is our job, especially as servant leaders, to acquire the ability to take a *long and loving look* at this congregation and to see it for the Holy Spirit-created miracle that it is. It

is the high and holy calling of pastors to shepherd the flock that the Holy Spirit has called together and to love the flock, know the flock, serve the flock, and to go through life with the flock - as fellow sinners and fellow followers of Christ.

† **Our local church family deserves our highest allegiance.**
Our common worship, our "meeting together," our service to one another, and our sustained mission of love to our neighbors - is not *part* of an "optional discipleship package" but rather is at the core of what it means to follow Christ together. Our long-term, rock solid, committed participation in our local church family is not part of an optional "extended warranty plan" above and beyond our personal ticket to heaven (or our personal relationship with Jesus) that we can choose or not choose to participate in when it fits our schedules, tastes, preferences, or feelings. Instead, it is at the heart of what God is doing in the world. The people of God, the church of God, is *always* God's main way of blessing/redeeming the world.

† **The church's main calling is to simply be the church.**
The church must simply be her weird, peculiar, patient, ordinary self. Nothing more, nothing less. She must commit herself to true worship and to disciple-making,

one at a time if necessary, putting people above programs, performance, and professional polish.

† **Your ordinary pastors are good for helping you take a long and loving look at your ordinary church.** Your shepherds should love you, know you, and go through life with you. Be patient with them. They are your brothers and sisters in the faith. They should love Christ and the Holy Scriptures, but they're also just trying, as you are, to get to heaven before they close the doors.

† **In all of my passions and convictions, I recognize that there are exceptions and extenuating circumstances.** In all things, grace and mystery prevail. Throughout history and throughout the world there are times and places that make it difficult to participate in a "regular" church family. There are times in a person's life that may lead to a "walkabout" for a season. There are three or four good reasons to leave a church or to change churches (and hundreds of bad reasons). There are a few good reasons to be temporarily "homeless," (i.e. to not have a regular church home for a while) and hundreds of bad reasons.

Epilogue

"There are no 'successful' congregations in Scripture or in the history of the church."

Eugene Peterson

Well, there it is. My love letter to the church - and to the only form it takes in the world: *congregation*. Local ordinary congregations. This is my love letter to my own congregation - and to yours. It's also my appeal, my dream, that our love, loyalty, and commitment to and for the local church, *our* local church, would grow. The message of this book, the passion of my heart, is hopefully simple:

> *My message is not new or fancy or sensational. It is most certainly not hip or cool. In the end, my message is not much more than a rediscovery that grandma was right all along: We all, indeed, should "go to church" and we should go to "our" church regularly, weekly, consistently. Please don't take this too harshly, but here's some good advice: find a church - hopefully a regular*

ordinary church that would be blessed to have you - and settle down. If you don't already have a home, start with the closest one, or the one that already has some of your most natural relationships: friends, family members, neighbors - but also one with plenty of people quite unlike you. Allow the Holy Spirit to make you part of a family. Pray for a sense of belonging and calling. Pray for a sense of "holy stuckness" wherein you follow Christ with your brothers and sisters, together through life, in loyal commitment to one another and with a deep sense of mutual accountability. Commit yourself to "hanging in there" with your church family, through thick and thin, for better or for worse, forgiving those who sin against you as they and God forgive you. Spend your life thanking God for the gift of community and for the miracle of a Holy Spirit created family. Allow your deep and abiding participation in this family to form your primary identity. Allow this fellowship to remain at the center of your allegiance to Christ and his body. Be assured that to follow Christ is to follow him together through life as part of a local congregation.

I'm not the only one who has written a love letter to the church. The Holy Scriptures are, in a very real sense, God's love letter and love song to the church, the bride of Christ. He says things in that love letter like:

"You are the body of Christ."

"You are my beautiful bride... without spot or wrinkle."

"You are as beautiful as Tirzah, my darling, as lovely as Jerusalem..."

Yes, God loves the church and will one day marry her.

She is his bride-to-be.

In return, the church responds:

I came from nothing.
I was nothing to look at.
All I can say is that He found me.
That's all I can say.

Somehow, someway, God loved me.
More amazing: somehow, someway,
God loved the whole world through me.

Look at me! I am sinful and have sinful children,
but I was made holy for my service - not for my own sake,
but for the sake of the world. I am immaculate as a bride,
beautiful to look upon because I have been purified.

He found me!
He found no other.
That is the reason for my humility, my pride, and my misery.
The song of my "happy fault"
is the hymn of salvation for the world.

- adapted from Arnold Stotzel

Afterword

Dr. Brad Jersak

CONFESSIONS OF A CRADLE CHURCHMAN

As a participant in Sunday services of an Eastern Orthodox congregation—a celebration we call "the Divine Liturgy"—I am a regular practitioner of the ancient tradition we call "confession." Indeed, confessing what troubles me to old Bishop Varlaam has become a liberating experience of grace, a lifeline for me. So, why not start there?

Here is my first confession: I'm a "cradle churchman." I was 20 years a Baptist before being called to pastoral ministry (Bethel Mennonite Church) and church planting (Fresh Wind Christian Fellowship). Today I serve as a reader and preacher in an Eastern Orthodox gathering.

In our era of "nones," "dones" and the #emptythepews exodus, I'm expected to be embarrassed about this. "Church," as Pastor Joe has beautifully described it, is something we're apparently supposed to admit to with a blush. And, of course, St. Paul's suspicion that "your meetings do more harm than good—and in part, I believe it" seems confirmed ad nauseum by ecclesial corruption across the centuries and to our day. To the critics and cynics, I generally nod unfazed and say, "Oh, believe me: it's worse than you think."

On the other hand, for all the vitriol against "organized" or "institutional church," I've also witnessed the mess and madness of disorganized and dispersed ex-church Christians. And yes, hierarchy (especially patriarchy) has surely earned the derision it endures. But if you think hierarchy's bad, try anarchy. But watch your back.

For those who've experienced the wounds of spiritual abuse and for whom exiting a congregation was a matter of survival, I'm so sorry. I won't presume to shame you back into those situations. That's not what I'm about. Nor is Joe.

In this book, Pastor Joe has modeled going back to the drawing board. What was this project called church—ekklesia—to its Founder Jesus Christ, or to Peter, Paul, James and John? What did they imagine it should be or could be? Just as importantly, what was church *not* and never meant to be? I'm so grateful for Joe's guidance through these questions. His words bear the authority of his experience.

AFTER DECONSTRUCTION

After deconstruction, some ex-churchies will discover they can't do this faith thing on their own. If the loneliness of post-communal faith sets in or when the cruelty of social media faith blindsides us, we may long for the incarnational church. We might pine for fellowship where the Word becomes flesh—with ordinary believers, with their warts and widows' casseroles included. There may yet be welcoming communities gathered to Christ, where we can touch and smell and feel empathy in real time for brothers and sisters.

If that day comes for you, I hope you'll live (or if necessary, move) within walking distance of an ordinary church like Amazing Grace and an ordinary shepherd like Pastor Joe. But whether you're on the verge of leaving church or pondering a return, I hope you've internalized the wisdom of this book.

I especially pray this for bewildered pastors and priests who stand watch at the revolving door of their ordinary fellowships (God LOVES ordinary churches). Take heart—Pastor Joe's ordinary story can be yours too. He's living proof that the ministry can be humbling but needn't be hellish, that leading can be serving without be lording, and a local ekklesia can be a hospital rather than a slaughterhouse. Thank you, my friend! You continue to guard my heart from despair—a Christlike church of wounded healers is possible and in fact, alive in this world.

REFLECTIONS ON "HOLDING DIFFERENCE"

For me, reading *Ordinary Church* stimulated further reflections and research. What follows are some of the trails I was compelled to explore.

First, Joe reminded me that church was never meant to be a fraternity of like-minded people who've arrived at spiritual sameness. Those who expect to live in the homogenous unison of a sterile, trigger-free "Jesus club" are forgetful of whom Christ invites to his table. If the Patriarchs and Apostles indicate a pattern, church is a family of diverse characters and temperaments, drawn from every class and category, inclusive of all (regardless of race, socio-economic status, gender, marital status, or political persuasions). "Being of one mind" is not conformity to a religious script but the shared humility of our common predicament (the broken human condition) and the shared hope of our single remedy (Christ and his gospel).

At the churches that I've pastored or attended, I see the very rich and extremely poor, the triathlete and the horrendously disabled, the newborn babe and the improbably old, the squeaky-clean puritan and the shame-filled penitent. They're weeping the same tears and receiving the same Cup. We're one family of God's beloved, earthy misfits, stepping on each other's toes and praying together, "Lord, have mercy." The Lord's Table is our great equalizer, where none are worthy and all are welcome to receive the divine medicine of our Great Physician.

In that atmosphere, maturity is the growing capacity to "hold difference" in mutual love and respect. It's seeing beyond our common ground to the real differences and understanding these as opportunities to love the other rather than fighting or excluding them.

In those moments, we're as close as we can get to "being church." We're gathered, but more than that, we're gathered "in his name." Whenever two or three (or two or three hundred) gather in Jesus' name, we're convening for more than a social event. We're together for a covenant gathering—we're an ekklesia.

EKKLESIA AS COVENANT GATHERING

Pastor Joe's comments on the biblical term ekklesia triggered my inner research assistant into deeper exploration. Much has been made of Christ and his apostles' choice of a term used for Roman civic assemblies—town hall gatherings if you will. While I'm familiar with that use in classical Greek, it seemed odd to me that Christ would opt to describe his new assemblies as ekklesia rather than employing the Jewish label "synagogue." It seems strange to think that Christ and the first believers would allow Hellenistic culture to overshadow their Jewish backstory as they conceived of their worship services.

Personally, I don't believe they did. I believe Protestant scholars have skipped over the use of ekklesia in the Septuagint

(LXX)—the Greek translation of the Hebrew Scriptures most cited in the New Testament. In its noun form, ekklesia is used 96 times in the LXX and 7 more times as a verb. It's a big mistake, in my view, to ignore how ekklesia was used with such great regularity in the Bible of the Apostles, as if they weren't informed by its specifically Jewish use! That oversight misses essential points in our language and theology.

As Joe points out, "In the LXX, … ekklesia never referred to Israel as a national unit. It always referred to an actual assembly or gathering of people. It did not designate an 'organization' or 'society.'"

This is exactly right: in the LXX, the Hebrew word qahal is translated into Greek primarily as ekklesia and also (but less frequently) rendered synagoge—thus, church and synagogue were often complementary synonyms. In English, qahal can also be translated assembly, congregation or even multitude.

When I systematically read through every occurrence of ekklesia in the LXX, taking note of recurring themes, I noticed a few important highlights:

The first use of ekklesia in the LXX is at Horeb, when the Lord spoke to Israel "on the day of the ekklesia" (Deut. 4:10). God commanded Moses to "gather" (ekklesiazein) the people to make his covenant with them (Deut. 5:2). Thereafter, that day was remembered as "the day of ekklesia" (Deut. 9:10, 18:16) and was reenacted in other sacred assemblies, such as when Moses' song is recited "in the hearing of the ekklesia of Israel" (Deut. 31:30). So too, when David announces that Solomon will build the Temple, he stands "in the midst of the ekkesia" (1 Chron. 28:2, 8; 29:1, 10, 20). And at the dedication of the Temple, Solomon blessed the ekklesia and prayed at the altar "before the ekklesia" (cf. 2 Chron. 6:3, 12-13; 7:8).

In case after case, ekklesia refers to the company of people gathered, sometimes generally but more specifically, in sacred assembly to hear or encounter God or God's spokesman (the ekklesiastes!). Ekklesia can then rightly be distilled to a covenant gathering of God and his people. Those who attend the ekklesia ARE the ekklesia. Those who didn't assemble were still regarded as the people of God or "children of Israel"—they're just not the ekklesia. They're the diaspora (dispersed) until they're gathered before God. In other words, God's people are always numbered either among the dispersed or the gathered.

All this tells speaks to me of something rich concerning the ekklesia. Yes, anyone can get together for dinner or bowling or drinks or battle. Sunagoge was used in that general way in the LXX—the enemy nations can assemble their armies as a sunagoge (company) to threaten Israel (e.g. Ezek. 38:4, 7, 13, 15). But while ekklesia sometimes refers to a crowd (LXX 1

Kgs. 17:47, Ps. 26:5), "the ekklesia of the Lord" is definitely a covenantal assembly, gathered to worship (2 Chron. 29:28-32), to appeal to God (2 Chron. 20:5), to inquire of the Lord (2 Chron. 1:5) or to repent before the Lord (Joel 2:16).

What are the implications for us as the NT ekklesia of Jesus Christ? It means that while individual Christ-followers are "in Christ" and baptized into his Body, one Christian does not constitute a church. Nor perhaps are all Christians actually "the church" while dispersed. We mystically become the ekklesia—the church—when we gather together locally to do church (ekklesiazein)—to proclaim and participate in the New Covenant of our Lord Jesus Christ.

That said, there is also a glorious and cosmic dimension to the ekklesia tied to and through the local gathering. Local assemblies are like portals to the church universal: visible and invisible (but never abstract). Hebrews 12 says that in Christ, we have come to Mount Zion, the New Covenant mountain, to the ekklesia of the firstborn, including all OT saints (from Heb. 11) and NT Christians, alive here and departed ("the spirits of the righteous ones made perfect"), to the myriads of angelic beings and to Christ himself. This is the ekklesia of God—cosmic in its inclusion and encompassing all of God's sentient beings from every covenant—but always uniquely experienced through the icon of actual people gathered for worship in the presence of God.

Whenever I enter a covenant gathering, I experience the universal church that only exists as and because it is instantiated in real flesh communities who love God and love each other.

I say all this because the Scriptures never regard the "universal church" as an abstraction sans actual people in community fellowship. Sure, you're probably still "saved" (whatever that means)—but apart from gathering, you're just not part of the ekklesia. In my tradition, we would say there is no universal church apart from actual people gathered to celebrate the covenant where Christ is visibly present in one another and in the Eucharist. That's ekklesia in my mind.

Again, I am grateful to Pastor Joe for taking us into the life of the church and sharing his life as a pastor (an ekklesiastes) in the greater breadth, depth and wisdom of his authentic shepherding experience. There's something about Joe's long and consistent faithfulness that gives his theology special integrity. A final thank you, my dear and ordinary friend: Pastor Joe.

Dr. Brad Jersak (PhD, Theology) is an author and teacher based in Abbotsford, BC. He serves as a reader and monastery preacher at All Saints of North America Orthodox Monastery. Brad is the author of several books including *A More Christlike God.*

I GIVE THANKS...

For Dr. Vernon Grounds, Eugene Peterson, and Gaylord Kindschy. You were my mentors in the pastoral vocation. You guided me along the good path and modeled what the life of a shepherd looks like. You were patient with me and allowed me to grow up slowly. To you and your legacy is this book dedicated.

For the congregation of Amazing Grace Church. For more than forty years, you have been much more of a pastor to me than I have been to you. You have taught me what it means to follow Christ - *together through life* – as the family of God on a mission, and as a creation of the Holy Spirit – a miracle that doesn't look much like a miracle. You have taught me all I know about love, acceptance, and forgiveness.

For my colleagues, theological buddies, heroes, and best friends in this shared calling: Brian and Peri Zahnd, Brad and Eden Jersak, Clifford and Kathy Brooks, Mercy Aiken, Derek and Jenni Vreeland, Gaylord and Sylvia Kindschy, Bryan and Debbie Peterson, John and Janet Zimmermann, Emily Zimmermann, Tim and Diane Ralph, Dave and Tyra Laughlin, Mike and Kristi Caulley, Philip and Janet Yancey, Scot McKnight, Dan Muzzy, John Oldfield, Les Avery, Jerry and Allegra Donaldson, Jim and Linda Sawyer, Craig and Janice Shannon, Gary and Becky Theander, Bryan Federowicz, Justin and Emily Pulford, Tim and Loree Pulford, Jack White, Stephanie White, Karen Reed, Rod and Lorraine Weimer, Jason and Ingrid Szolomayer, Glen and Sara Guenther, David McDonald, Bob Mossman, Tom Buxton, and Maddie Keith, who *"like Botticelli's niece, was always there as I painted my masterpiece"* (I had to sneak Dylan in one more time). Thanks for pushing me to finish this thing. Thanks for prohibiting me from using the subtitle: *"Get your blessed assurance to church or burn forever!"*

For my co-pastors over the years (Gaylord, Chuck, Steve, Jan, Sam, and John): I can't imagine what it must have been like to minister next to me! Thanks for your patience and forbearance. **And for our faithful church secretaries and co-workers**, LaVaughn Gillespie and Cheri Gardner, for your invaluable help, daily support, proofreading, and constant encouragement.

For my mother, Norma Jean Hough, and grandmother, Irma B. Humason, through whom came my faith in Jesus Christ, my passion for Christ's church, and my first crazy thoughts about being a pastor someday - and my supportive siblings: Kris and Kelly Spickler, Mike and Sallie Galloway, Brian Beach, Gaylan and Suzanne Kindschy, and Sharon Kindschy. *To Kris Spickler, a special thanks for your constant* *support and encouragement. You literally saved my life more than once.*

For my encouraging friends and family that left me way too soon: my dad Stan Beach, Vernon Grounds, Eugene and Jan Peterson, Dick Gilbert, Robin Kendzior, Chuck VanderKooi, LaVaughn Gillespie, and many others. I apologize for dragging my feet and not finishing this book sooner.

For the First Things First group: Dean and Jill, Mark, Sally, Max (may his soul rest in peace), Wayne, Juliane, Linda, Mac, Jim, John from the mountains, Charmane, Chuck, Keith, Allie, Lisa, and all of the rest of you ragamuffins.

For Mike Philips and Marcia Beach, for pushing me to write this thing (for forty years) and for helping me make it happen with your prayers and generous financial support.

For Jason Swan Clark, Brian Zahnd, Brad Jersak, Jerry Donaldson, and Jim Sawyer for reading and endorsing the book.

For Stacey Lane for her wonderful design work on the book, both inside and out.

For my children, Aaron and Mallory, Adam and Brittany, my "mini-me" Andrew, and my other mini-me: my daughter

Alicia and Thomas. You all really do "get it." You totally get the message of my heart and life. Everything I write about in this book – you've understood and you've been living it out on a daily basis. My passionate thoughts about the local church – you have somehow both shaped them and absorbed them and then transformed them into a way of life. You make the Jesus Way seem like the only way to live. Your daily commitment to the Lord, to your church family, to your parents, and to each other is my greatest joy.

For my grandsons, Avram Stanley, Silas James, Jonathan Francis, Levi Joseph, Maximillion Kolbe, **and my granddaughters** Charlie Anne, Marion Charis, and Josephine Frances (and any future grandchildren). You're all too young to know or care about your "Papa Beach's" theological convictions about the local church. All you care about is being with me, knowing that your Papa loves you beyond words, and that your church is your family. Maybe that's all our Heavenly Father wants us to know. I want nothing more than for the church, hopefully *this church*, to be here for you as you grow up. I want you to have the same precious gift that we have had. I want you to be able to go *together through life* with an actual multi-generational church family. I want a church to be here for my children and my children's children - a church that is faithful to Christ, committed to each other in loyal love, and passionate about serving her neighbors.

For my wife, Karen. I often wonder what you were thinking when, as a young girl, having no clue as to what you were doing, you committed yourself to go *together through life* with an "under-developed" ski racer with a backpack full of issues. I'm sure that you've often wondered the same thing. And I do mean *often*. Thanks for hanging in there through the ups and downs and all arounds and for hanging on to the hope that, by God's grace, maybe just maybe, the best is yet to be and that, maybe just maybe, I would one day, finally, finish this book!

NOTES

FOREWORD

v *Shelter From the Storm*: Bob Dylan, Special Rider Music, 1975.

CHAPTER ONE: *INTRODUCTION TO THE ORDINARY CHURCH*

1 *When Hauerwas writes about the church:* William T. Cavanaugh, *Migrations of the Holy: God, State, and the Political Meaning of the Church* (Grand Rapids, MI: Eerdmans, 2011), 192.

5 *I failed to love what was present and decided to love what was possible instead:* Kate Bowler, *Everything Happens for a Reason: And Other Lies I've Loved* (New York, N.Y.: Random House, 2018), 156.

8 *Eleusis*: Gerhard Lohfink, *Does God Need The Church* (Collegeville, MN: Liturgical Press, 1999), 253-254.

CHAPTER TWO: *THE STATE OF THE UNION*

14 *My dear Wormwood:* C. S. Lewis, *Screwtape Letters* (New York, N.Y.: Macmillan, 1978), Chapter 16

18 M*aybe it's the failure of the church – the Catholic church's abuse scandals, evangelical's politicization, mainliner's lukewarmness:* Timothy P. Carney, *Alienated America: Why Some Places Thrive While Other Places Collapse* (New York, N.Y.: HarperCollins, 2019), 123.

18 *The unchurching of America is at the root of America's*

economic and social problems: Ibid., 122.

19 *Turns out I identify more with Maria from The Sound of Music.* Sam Eaton. https://faithit.com/12-reasons-millennials-over-church-sam-eaton/

21 *Most of the influential Christian leaders do not attend church:* Don Miller's famous blog and his follow-up blog have been removed and you will now be re-directed to his Story Brand website. I don't blame him. You'll just have to trust me on this one. You can still find countless references and responses to his blogs which contain all the quotes to which I'm referring.

22 *Today, many churches look like night clubs.* Don Miller. See above.

23 The original and infamous Kevin Miller article. (Since removed). https://www.christianitytoday.com/pastors/2014/february-online-only/strange-yet-familiar-tale-of-brian-rob-and-don.html

25 *Should spending twenty-four years as a church planter qualify one as a quitter:* Brian McLaren, https://www.patheos.com/blogs/brianmclaren/2014/02/qr-you-rob-bell-donald-miller-and-christianity-today/

25 *It turns out that we evangelicals need a loftier ecclesiology*: Kevin Miller's original article. See above.

27 *In the end, all we have is the church*: Rachel Held Evans, *Searching For Sunday: Loving, Leaving, and Finding the Church* (Nashville, TN: Nelson Books, 2015), 256.

27 *The tangible, tactile nature of the sacraments*: Rachel Held Evans, Ibid., xvi

29 *Keep the Church Weird*: Rachel Held Evans, https://www.youtube.com/results?search_query=rachel+held+evans+keep+the+church+weird

33 *Barna's enthusiasm for the First Church of the Individual raises troubling questions.* Kevin Miller. See above.

33 *George Barna did that study about "radical" Christians.* Scot

McKnight. Interview by Leslie Leyland Fields. https://www.youtube.com/watch?v=VEKLFtAKxJ4&t=327s

34 *I would say that when young people say that they value "community:"* Ibid.

34 *Our Christian subculture is marked by church hopping:* Alissa Wilkinson, *Why Pop Culture Is Obsessed with 'Identity'* (Christianity Today, Dec. 28, 2015).

35 *We have to return to the roots of our faith*: Rod Dreher, *The Benedict Option: A Strategy For Christians in a Post-Christian Nation* (New York, N.Y.: Penguin Random House, 2017), 3.

39 *Your idea of comunity, to my ears, honestly, sounds more American and Romantic:* Jonathan Leeman. https://www.thegospelcoalition.org/article/dear-donald-miller/

41 *Want to become a revolutionary? Here's my counsel*: Kevin Miller, see above.

43 *I practiced the radical spiritual art of staying put*: Sarah Bessey, *Out of Sorts: Making Peace With an Evolving Faith* (New York, N.Y., Simon and Schuster, 2015), 95.

44 *This is not work for the faint of heart:* Ibid., 96

44 *I want my tinies to know what my voice sounds like when I sing Amazing Grace:* Ibid., 102.

CHAPTER THREE: *THE CHURCH IN THE CHURCH'S SCRIPTURE*

45 *Common worship… is the sine qua non* of being a Christian*:* Fleming Rutledge. http://www.patheos.com/blogs/jesuscreed/2018/02/10/interview-fleming-rutledge/#comment-3752586574

45 *I wish Martin Luther's wish had come true and that in our creeds and confessions:* Karl Barth, *Dogmatics In Outline*, trans. G. T. Thomson (London, Great Britain: SCM Press, 1949), 141. Barth's exact words (translated) were: *It would be great gain, could Luther's urgent desire have been carried out and the word 'congregation'*

had taken the place of the word 'church.'

47 *One of the great problems of Evangelical life in America:* Stanley Hauerwas. *Transcript: Nearing the End – A Conversation with Theologian Stanley Hauerwas* (April 28, 2014). https://www.patheos.com/blogs/paperbacktheology/2014/05/hauerwas-and-mohler-notes-from-an-unlikely-conversation.html

55 *Church:* Peter O'Brien, *IVP's Dictionary of Paul and His Letters* (Downers Grove, IL: IVP, 1993).

57 *It is best not to apply the idea of invisibility to the Church:* Karl Barth, *Dogmatics In Outline*, 142

60-61 *I resist the trend toward megachurches, preferring smaller places out of the spotlight:* Philip Yancey, "Why I Don't Attend a Megachurch." https://www.christianitytoday.com/ct/1996/may20/6t6080.html

65 *In other words, Don, the main thing I want to highlight in response to both of your posts.* Jonathan Leeman, https://www.thegospelcoalition.org/article/dear-donald-miller/

CHAPTER FOUR: *AMAZING GRACE CHURCH*

67 *The only thing I want in life is to be known for loving Christ, to build his church, to love his bride: Kari Jobe, The Cause of Christ (Sparrow).*

67-68 *It is interesting to note that Jesus, who in abridged form is quite popular with the non-church crowd, was not anti-institutional:* Eugene Peterson, *The Jesus Way: A Conversation on the Ways That Jesus is the Way* (Grand Rapids, MI: Eerdmans Publishing, 2007), 230-232.

77 *I ask no dream, no prophet ecstasies:* old hymn quoted by Fred Craddock, "Dr. Fred Craddock on a Preacher's Calling," https://www.youtube.com/watch?v=nvCOqif13Zo

101 *Let us honor her, because she is the bride of so great a Lord. And what am I to say?* Augustine. *The Works of Saint Augustine: Sermons III/6 (New Rochelle, N.Y.: New City Press, 1993), Sermon 213, p 145*

101 *I could believe in Christ if he did not drag behind him his leprous bride, the Church.* From the romantic poet Southey, as quoted by William Willimon, *What's Right With the Church* (New York, N.Y.: Harper and Row, 1985), 3. The full quote is worthwhile. It continues: *Jesus had many admirers who feel that he married beneath his station. They love Christ but are unable to love those whom he has loved.*

CHAPTER FIVE: *HEALTH CLUB, HALF-WAY HOUSE, HOSPITAL, OR HOME?*

111 *The quickest way to get home is to stay there:* Zack Eswine, *Sensing Jesus: Life and Ministry as a Human Being* (Wheaton, IL: Crossway, 2013), 86.

112 *We should leave a worship service asking ourselves not 'what did I get out of it:'* Philip Yancey, *Church: Why Bother?: My Personal Pilgrimage* (Grand Rapids, MI: Zondervan, 1998), 24-25.

112 *There are two things we cannot do alone: Paul Tournier as quoted by Yancey,* Ibid., 37.

114 *Some of my greatest wounds have come from church*: Bessey, 103.

114 *There was a man in Denver named Gene Cisneros who ran a health club.* https://www.denverpost.com/2010/07/07/gene-cisneros-is-denvers-no-frills-philospher-of-fitness/

127 *The room smelled of hand lotion and chewing gum:* Heather Kopp, *Sober Mercies: How Love Caught Up With a Christian Drunk* (New York, N.Y.: Hachette Book Group, 2013), 79.

129 *Man is born broken. He lives by mending. The grace of God is glue*: Eugene O'Neil as quoted by Ernest Kurtz, *The Spirituality of Imperfection: Storytelling and the Search for Meaning*: (New York, N.Y.: Random House, 1992),

134 *I'm thrilled whenever Christians are hungry for God's Word, but sermon podcasts should be a "snack" or "side," not the "main dish:* Pastor Kwan, Christianity Today, April 20, 2018, https://www.

christianitytoday.com/ct/2018/may/should-pastors-podcast-their-sermons.html

134 *We should all still find ourselves accountable to a local congregation with local incarnate relationship-based authority*: Skye Jethani, https://www.youtube.com/watch?v=6bkTYhOoRfM

CHAPTER SIX: *WHEN THE CHURCH WAS A FAMILY*

137 *When the church was a family, the church was on fire:* Joseph Hellerman, *When the Church Was a Family: Recapturing Jesus' Vision for Authentic Christian Community* (Nashville, TN: B&H Publishing Group, 2009), 229.

139 *The New Testament picture of the church as a family*: Ibid., 7.

140 *Spiritual formation occurs in the context of community.* Ibid. 1.

142 *People who stay also grow*: Ibid., 1

142 *It is a simple but profound biblical reality that we both grow and thrive together or we do not grow much at all*: Ibid., 1

142 *The quickest way to get home is to stay there*: Eswine, 86.

142 *Our Christian subculture is marked by church hopping,* Alissa Wilkinson, see above.

143 *We've been socialized to believe*: Hellerman, 4.

143 *The radical spiritual art of staying put*: Bessey, 95.

144 *Because by faith there is more to... these local people with their daily stories:* Eswine, 53.

144 *The radical act of staying put is shaping me*: Bessey, 119.

145 *Pope John Paul II and Pope Benedict XVI defined the church as a "Communio of Disciples in Mission:" from a personal talk by George Weigel at Holy Name Catholic Church, Sheridan, CO., a summary of the same talk can be found at*: https://www.patheos.com/blogs/scottericalt/the-church-is-a-communion-of-disciples-in-

mission/

146 *It's about communion. It's about baptism. It's about confession:* Rachel Held Evans, *Keep The Church Weird*, see above.

147 *Aristotle said that the best activities are the most useless:* Robert Barron, *Catholicism: A Journey to the Heart of the Faith* (New York, N.Y.: Random House, 2011), 172.

148 *We play football and we play musical instruments because*: Barron, Ibid., 172-173.

150-152 *Not youth church, or contemporary church, or postmodern church. Just plain, boring, ordinary church:* Mike Yaconelli, from an early Youthworker Journal article. You can find it in his collected words: *Getting Fired for the Glory of God* (Grand Rapids, MI: Zondervan, 2008), 93-94. (Youth Specialties).

153 *I grew up in one of those big ol' megachurches you're talking about*, Jonathan Aigner, https://www.patheos.com/blogs/ponderanew/2016/03/03/dont-take-your-kids-to-a-megachurch-an-open-letter-to-andy-stanley/

158 *Go to the nearest smallest church and commit yourself to being there for 6 months*: Eugene Peterson, http://jonathanmerritt.religionnews.com/2013/09/27/faithful-end-interview-eugene-peterson/#sthash.3GZ6omsl.dpuf

CHAPTER SEVEN: *FIRST CHURCH OF THE INDIVIDUAL*

159 *The tune of radical individualism has been playing in our ears*: Joseph Hellerman, 4.

161 *There was a famous religious shrine in the ancient world at a place called* Eleusis: Lohfink, 253-254.

165 *Dreher tells the story of how he and his family moved back to his small hometown:* Dreher, 67.

166 *Not everyone is called to return to their hometown, of course, but everybody should think deeply about the spiritual and emotional costs:* Ibid.

166 *My wife and I took stock of how much we and our children had grown in faith:* Ibid., 131.

167 *Why be close? Because, as I said earlier, the church can't just be the place you go on Sundays:* Ibid.

168 *My Church*: Maren Morris (2016 Sony Music Entertainment)

169 *Jesus banded them into a flock, a society, a church*: Frank Sheed, *Theology and Sanity* (San Francisco, CA: Ignatius Press, 1946), 291.

170 *The internal stories are often these: 'I need a break:* Jason Swan Clark. "You Don't Need to Go to Church to be a Christian and other fairy tales." https://www.patheos.com/blogs/jesuscreed/2019/01/22/81613/

172 *We are people who normally would not mix: The Big Book of Alcoholics Anonymous*, 17.

173 *God is not fastidious in the company he keeps*: Eugene Peterson, *Practice Resurrection: A Conversation on Growing Up In Christ* (Grand Rapids, MI: Eerdmans, 2010), 181.

CHAPTER EIGHT: *THE PATIENT FERMENT OF THE ORDINARY CHURCH*

177 *Church growth strategies are the death gurgle of a church that has lost its way.* Stanley Hauerwas. This oft-quoted line was originally an endorsement blurb on: Timothy Scuttle, *Shrink: Faithful Ministry in a Church-Growth Culture* (Grand Rapids, MI: Zondervan, 2014).

177 *The key to the obedience of God's people is not their effectiveness but their patience:* John Howard Yoder, *The Politics of Jesus* (Grand Rapids, MI: Eerdmans, 1972), 232.

178 *The Christian assembly was not one of a palette of social commitments:* Alan Kreider, *The Patient Ferment of the Early Church: The Improbable Rise of Christianity in the Roman Empire* (Grand Rapids, MI: Baker, 2016), 60.

181 *We have a huge advertising industry designed to stir up appetites*: Eugene Peterson, *The Jesus Way*, 6.

183 *FAST is: busy, controlling… SLOW is: Calm, careful:* C. Christopher Smith and John Pattison, *Slow Church: Cultivating Community in the Patient Way of Jesus* (Downers Grove, IL: IVP, 2014), 13.

184 *The fast-food culture of this country is an apt metaphor for the state of the church:* Brennan Manning in a personal comment from Brennan in a small group I attended with him.

185 *Playlands bring in children, who bring in parents, who bring in money:* Eric Schlosser, *Fast Food Nation: The Dark Side of the All-American Meal* (New York, N.Y.: Houghton Mifflin: 2001), 47.

186 *Future historians, I hope, will consider the American fast food industry a relic of the twentieth century:* Ibid.

187 *One of the ways modernity captured Christianity was in this area of mission:* Brian McLaren, *A New Kind of Christian: A Tale of Two Friends on a Spiritual Journey* (San Francisco, CA: Jossey-Bass: 2001), 224.

188 *God, shrink our territory, and narrow our boundaries:* Smith and Pattison, 44.

189 *We need wines [and churches] that have birth certificates:* Terry Theiese, *Reading Between the Vines* (Berkeley, CA: University of California, 2010), 32.

190 *The smartest thing a cellarmaster [or pastor] can know is the right time… to do nothing.* Ibid., 53.

194 *It was by consensus that the Quakers in the early years of the United States became the first religious community to reject the practice of slavery*: Pattison and Smith, 217.

195 *I'm sorry if I sound bitter. I'm not, really. More relieved than anything else*: Jonathan Aigner, https://www.patheos.com/blogs/ponderanew/2018/08/10/5088/ (aug 10 2018) "Farewell, Willow Creek: Where the "Regular" Churches Can Go From Here"

196 *So, church, it's time to rediscover your sacred, holy identity:*

Ibid.

197 Thankfully, I restrained myself when sarcastically describing the best and fastest way to grow a church nowadays. For a while there, I was tempted to say: Find an interesting location, hire a gifted CEO, get some black walls and create a comfortable enticing atmosphere that conveys a certain vibe, secure a world-class band complete with fog machine and world class lighting and sound, find some attractive singers with phenomenal voices that know how to look spiritual and worship-full and, most of all, get yourself a gifted, attractive, charismatic "senior teaching pastor" – preferably a man, preferably in his early 40's, preferably buff so he can wear a tight shirt and hopefully show off his tattoo, preferably in tight jeans, preferably with some holes in the knees, and make sure he's a gifted orator and storyteller, make sure his messages are funny but also bring a few tears – but most importantly make sure his messages are user-friendly and relevant and help people have happy lives and happy marriages and happy children and happy finances. But, far be it for me to be sarcastic, so I toned it down quite a bit.

CHAPTER NINE: *SANDBARS AND BACKPACKS*

220 *He Don't Live Here No More*: Robbie Robertson (How To Become Clairvoyant by Robbie Robertson 2011, 429 Records)

CHAPTER TEN: *THE ORDINARY PASTOR OF AN ORDINARY CHURCH*

221 *We have trouble finding the church, not because it is invisible:* Eugene Peterson, Practice Resurrection, 26.

222 *So why do I go to church? Because… we know and love our pastors for their humanity:* Bessey, 101.

222 *I realized that this was my place and work in the church:* Eugene Peterson, *Practice Resurrection*, 27.

224 *I made more than my share of mistakes [during my first pastorate]:* Lewis Smedes, *My God and I: A Spiritual Memoir* (Grand Rapids, MI: 2003), *108-109.*

224 *Every once in a while, a shaft of blazing beauty seems to break out of nowhere*: Eugene Peterson, *Leap Over a Wall: Earthy Spirituality for Everyday Christians* (San Francisco, CA: HarperSanFrancisco, 1997), 101.

226 Rich Mullins tells a story about some young Christians: Rich Mullins (Family Broadcasting Corporation Seminar, 1994) https://www.youtube.com/watch?v=WTnBsPdUuuk&t=1077s

229 *Sometimes I wonder how Jesus would have fared in this day of mass media and high-tech ministry*: Yancey, *"Why I Don't Attend a Megachurch."* See above.

233 *In this sense, God hates visionary dreaming,* Dietrich Bonhoeffer, *Life Together, trans. John Doberstein* (San Francisco, CA: Harper and Row: 1954), 27.

234 *A pastor should not complain about his congregation, certainly never to other people, but also not even to God:* Ibid., 29.

237 *God loves you. He's on your side. He's coming after you. He's relentless:* Leif Peterson. Eugene Peterson's Memorial Service. Used by permission from the family.

CHAPTER ELEVEN: *FRONT ROW SEATS*

239 *I simply continue to be amazed by how easily we leave our local church:* Sean Palmer, *Unarmed Empire: In Search of Beloved Community* (Eugene, OR: Wipf and Stock, 2017), 11.

251 *Two or three of the ladies had pronounced views on points of doctrine:* Marilynne Robinson, *Gilead* (New York, N.Y.: Farrar, Straus, and Giroux, 2004), 208.

EPILOGUE

261 *There are no successful congregations:* Eugene Peterson, *Practice Resurrection*, 29.

262 This final poem, ending with: *The song of my "happy fault is the hymn of salvation for the world:* adapted from Arnold Stotzel as quoted by Lohfink, 321-322.

SOME BOOKS THAT SHAPED MY LIFE AND THIS BOOK

1. **Everything written by Eugene Peterson. Especially:**

    Under the Unpredictable Plant

    Working the Angles

    The Pastor

    The Subversive Pastor

    Leap Over a Wall

    The Jesus Way

    Christ Plays in Ten Thousand Places

    Five Smooth Stones for Pastoral Work

2. **Everything written by Philip Yancey. Especially:**

    Church: Why Bother?

    What's So Amazing About Grace?

    The Jesus I Never Knew

    Soul Survivor

3. **Everything written by N.T. Wright. Especially:**

    Surprised by Hope

    Simply Jesus

    How God Became King

    Simply Good News

    The Day the Revolution Began

4. **Everything written by Brian Zahnd. Especially:**

Unconditional

Beauty Will Save the World

Water to Wine

5. **Everything written by Scot McKnight. Especially:**

The King Jesus Gospel

Kingdom Conspiracy

A Community of Differents

6. **Gerhard Lohfink**.

Does God Need the Church?

7. **William Willimon**.

What's Right With the Church

Resident Aliens. (with Stanley Hauerwas)

8. **Stanley Hauerwas**.

Hannah's Child.

9. **Rodney Clapp**.

A Peculiar People.

10. **C. Christopher Smith and John Pattison**.

Slow Church.

11. **Zack Eswine**.
Sensing Jesus
(and it's shorter revision, The Imperfect Pastor).

12. **Rod Dreher**.
The Benedict Option.

13. **Sarah Bessey**.
Out of Sorts.

14. **Sean Palmer**.
Unarmed Empire.

15. **Jonathan Aigner** and **Jason Swan Clark**.
All blogs, articles, and books by either.

ABOUT THE AUTHOR

Joe Beach lives in Morrison, Colorado, and is one of the pastors at Amazing Grace Church in the southwest area of Denver, Colorado. Joe grew up in Central California and spent the first twenty-four years of his life travelling the world while pursuing Olympic dreams as an Alpine Ski Racer. After reaching a national ranking in the top fifteen racers (in Giant Slalom), Joe raced for the University of Denver, earning MVP honors each season. After retiring from racing, Joe married, attended Denver Seminary, entered full-time pastoral ministry, and had four children.

Joe has been married to Karen for thirty-seven years and his four children who are now all adults (ages 25-35). Three are married with children and Joe now has eight grandchildren (and counting). Joe has also enjoyed a career on the side as a high school coach (Boys' Tennis, Baseball, and Soccer).

Joe is an avid reader, wannabe writer, armchair theologian, amateur dylanologist, fair-to-middling pastor/preacher, tournament tennis player, baseball lover, mediocre flyfisherman, lousy golfer, beginner cyclist, Philip Yancey's ski buddy, occasional mountain climber, wannabe chef, kombucha brewer, Mexican food connoisseur, live kidney donor (2001), Enneagram Type Seven (a party looking for a place to happen… but struggles mightily with self-discipline), and cheese lover. Other than that, he's fairly boring and is pretty much a walking disaster, hanging on to God's grace with all he has, and trying to get to heaven before they close the door.

Contact: ohmercy5@gmail.com

Amazing Grace Church: agcdenver.net

Joseph Beach on Twitter: @joethepastor

Printed in Great Britain
by Amazon